Working with the Impulsive Person

Working with the Impulsive Person

Edited by

Howard A. Wishnie

Harvard Medical School at
The Cambridge Hospital
Cambridge, Massachusetts
and
Bedford Veterans Administration Hospital
Bedford, Massachusetts

and

Joyce Nevis-Olesen

The Judge Baker Guidance Center
Boston, Massachusetts

Plenum Press · New York and London

Library of Congress Cataloging in Publication Data

Main entry under title:

Working with the impulsive person.

Proceedings of the conference held in Cambridge, Mass., March 5—6, 1977.
Includes index.
1. Impulsive personality — Congresses. I. Wishnie, Howard. II. Nevis-Olesen, Joyce.
[DNLM: 1. Personality disorders — Congresses. 2. Impulsive behavior — Congresses.
WM190 W 926 1977]
RC569.5.I46W67   616.8'58   79-13899
ISBN 0-306-40184-3

Proceedings of the Conference held in Cambridge, Massachusetts, March 5—6, 1977.

© 1979 Plenum Press, New York
A Division of Plenum Publishing Corporation
227 West 17th Street, New York, N.Y. 10011

Printed in the United States of America

Preface

The development of the material in this volume began
with a realization by the staff at The Cambridge-Somerville
Mental Health and Retardation Center (in the Massachusetts
cities of Cambridge and Somerville) that an increasing number of people were entering the mental health system with
problems related to the very nature of their personalities.
A significant number of these people presented issues that
had not been identified previously within the spectrum of
psychiatric treatment. Such issues as marital discord involving impulsive and violent behavior toward spouses or
children, drug abuse, alcoholism, brawling, and so forth were
increasingly being viewed as symptomatic of disruptions in
an individual's emotional makeup. These people usually did
not seek treatment; their problems were most often managed
by courts and social welfare agencies. In fact, we were not
clear as to what constituted the best treatment.

The conference on which this book is based was conceived
of as an attempt to bring together people of varying backgrounds to discuss in a general, nontechnical fashion the
approaches they have tried in working with such people. We
attempted to bridge the gap between the many sophisticated
theorists who work in this area and the front-line personnel
who daily confront these problems. Because of the general
scope of the conference, the papers covered a wide range of
issues and experiences.

Our definition of impulsive persons was, simply: those
people whose behavior is habitually characterized by poorly
planned actions, hastily conceived, and carried out in such
a manner that the results are frequently more distressful for
the individual than his initial situation. Such people live
in chronic chaos unless stability is imposed by others. The
breadth of this definition was used purposely to allow the
conference to touch on many areas. The premature classification of impulsive people into subgroups based on their most
troubling or recent symptom has a basic problem. It helps

us to categorize such people but it shortcircuits our thinking. Wilhelm Reich took this up in 1925 in his monograph on
the impulsive character: "The basic flaw in such attempts
[classification by single symptoms] is that a single outstanding trait becomes the yardstick for classification in
the group; what is overlooked is the fact, for example, that
every impulsive (in Bleuler's sense) is as unstable as he is
perverted; that every pervert is antisocial and also, therefore, a troublemaker."

The series of papers presented here delineates the clinical and research experience of their authors focused on people with impulse-ridden personalities. Our aim is to call
attention to the origins, dynamics, and attitudes encountered
in attempting to work with these people--a population often
overlooked and considered beyond help.

Howard A. Wishnie, M.D.
Cambridge, Massachusetts
1978

Contents

III: THE IMPULSIVE PATIENT AND THE
       CRIMINAL JUSTICE SYSTEM

IV: HISTORICAL OVERVIEW AND
      FUTURE ISSUES

Part I

Etiological Foundations

PSYCHODYNAMICS OF IMPULSIVE BEHAVIOR

Gerald Adler, M.D.

Professor of Psychiatry and Director of Training in Adult Psychiatry, Tufts University School
of Medicine, Boston, Massachusetts

In discussing treatment of patients with impulsive disorders, we can take one of two positions: (1) that we know
too little and are thus helpless to treat many of them successfully (based on recidivist and outcome studies); or
(2) that we know more than we realize and our failures lie
in the complexities of applying what we know. The actual
situation most often lies somewhere between the poles of
these two views, but for purposes of discussion I want to
examine, support, and perhaps overemphasize how much we know
and how much our theoretical knowledge is gradually increasing. I shall also attempt to provide a theoretical framework for treatment of impulse-ridden patients in a variety
of settings and ask why it is so difficult to apply what we
know effectively to clinical situations.

Those who have worked with impulsive or impulse-ridden
patients know that as a group they range across a wide and
varied diagnostic spectrum--from neurotics who may act out
a very specific conflict under intense and specific stress,
to those with primitive character disorders, to psychotics
whose impulsivity is a gross manifestation of disorganization. Yet a denominator common to all appears to exist:
almost all the impulsive acts of this large group of patients
have specific interpersonal communicative effects--the turning to a family, a therapist or, ultimately, especially in
the more severe manifestations, to society for help in controlling impulses and feelings that have become overwhelming
(Bernabeau, 1958).

Impulsivity can be viewed from different but overlapping vantage points: as a manifestation of a person's inability to contain unbearable impulses, affects, or conflicts; as an indication of defective ego and superego functioning; as evidence of developmental failure; as an aspect of faulty self-esteem regulation; or as a communication for help. While this paper focuses on the individual and the family as the context for the psychodynamics of these internal mechanisms, cultural values and conflicts are also of critical importance. In working with impulse-ridden patients, the complex therapeutic issues that arise not infrequently have crucial sociocultural dimensions requiring knowledge, understanding, and acceptance.

The psychiatric and psychoanalytic literature over the past two decades has increased our theoretical understanding of impulse-ridden patients. This most recent knowledge helps us articulate more clearly the intuitive skills of gifted clinicians, exemplified in Aichhorn's pioneering work conducted in 1925 and first published in 1935. I shall discuss some of these theoretical concepts because I believe they are clinically useful, whether we work in private offices, hospitals, courts, community clinics, or prisons. I shall stress impulsivity in more primitive patients since they more readily and clearly highlight the theoretical and clinical issues.

The description of impulse-ridden patients as people who have ego or superego defects is derived from a conceptual framework postulating that certain "structures" or functions are either absent in these patients or have been lost during the turmoil of regression. In clinical terms, people with defective ego structures chronically put their feelings and impulses into action, or regress to impulsive behavior as a result of certain stresses. Similar statements may be made about individuals with superego defects. For example, in prisons we see inmates whose histories seem to lack any evidence of superego functions during episodes of dangerous impulsivity, as instanced by the inmate who reported that during an armed robbery he would have no hesitation in shooting anyone "dumb enough" to try to stop him: he was "entitled" to get what he wanted and would feel no guilt or remorse if he had to kill someone who interferred.

Our attempts to understand the fluctuating ego and superego functioning of more primitive impulsive patients have

led to an examination of the possible relevance of childhood
developmental issues to these defects. We turn to child
development data in particular to understand what permits
some children to have experiences that become constructive
as they become permanent--that is, experiences introjected
so that adequate ego and superego development occurs--in
contrast to those whose experiences yield the ego and superego defects found in primitive impulse-ridden patients.
A significant literature describes environmental factors in
the early lives of a large number of impulse-ridden patients
that have failed to provide appropriate support and adult
models for ultimate identification. Many such persons come
from broken homes where violence and impulsivity are part of
everyday life. Familiar patterns include: fathers who are
absent or alcoholic; mothers who are depressed, inconsistent,
and emotionally unavailable; or families that are superficial-
ly intact but nonetheless harbor these problem themes in
latent form, which the child then experiences (Robins, 1966).

The contributions of Winnicott (1965) and Mahler (1971,
1972) are useful in elaborating the developmental issues
upon which such familial deprivation and inconsistency impinge. Winnicott has brought the concepts "good-enough
mothering" and "the holding environment" into our vocabulary.
He defined, in mother-child terms, what Hartmann (1939) called
"the average, expectable environment" necessary for healthy
ego development. Winnicott emphasized the empathic bond between mother and child, the expectation that failures in this
empathy would occur, and the broad limits of what might be
"good enough." Part of the usefulness of Winnicott's contribution is that he brought a human, understandable, deceptive-
ly simple interactional framework into a literature abound-
ing in a complex metapsychology that was difficult for most
clinicians to grasp, much less use. His concepts helped
bridge the gap between those of child development theory and
theories of interpersonal and object relations. In addition,
it provided a framework for understanding some of the necessary conditions whereby the external world and the child's
interactions with others become a permanent part of the
child's self-concept.

Winnicott's "holding environment" concept is particularly relevant to a discussion of impulsive patients. As
an extension of his notion of "good-enough mothering," this
concept focuses on provision of sufficient support by the

important people in the child's life, at each developmental
level, to help the child feel safely held.

Many impulsive persons, whether children or adults,
will run away from a situation that provides "holding," yet
simultaneously long for it. In Semrad's terms (1969), some
patients "arrange it for themselves"--that is, act so that
they are held and contained (in courts and prisons)--as a
consequence of their impulsivity and their running because
they have actually wanted this "holding." In case histories
we find evidence that many of these patients lacked what we
would call satisfactory holding environments in childhood.
They then relive--either with therapists in the transference
or with society through its agencies--the distrust, anger, and
disappointment with valued persons, whom they have often
idealized and with whom they have often felt disappointment. The running away as part of the impulsivity can be
interpreted in a number of ways: as a manifestation of
anger; as an attempt to avoid engulfment or mutual destruction that may be fantasied if holding and containment occur; or as a wish to be contained, held, and protected.

Mahler (1971, 1972) describes the developmental subphases that lead from symbiosis to separation-individuation,
culminating in the child's capacity to maintain, as a separate individual, an emotional tie to the mother, who is remembered even in the face of frustration. Two of these sub-
phases--the practicing and the rapprochement--may be particularly relevant in relation to Winnicott's concepts.

Mahler places the practicing subphase at the beginning
of the small child's ability to walk--a time during which
the child is particularly curious, delighted with his new
discoveries, and oblivious to the world's hazards as he
wanders about and explores. It is also a time when empathic
parents must watch and protect the child from obvious dangers, and yet not constrict and stifle prematurely his
enthusiasm for exploration. The developmental histories
from parents of patients with impulsive problems often
describe this "practicing" period as a time when their child
was already running away from them. Although some of these
children may be hyperactive, due to complex and interacting
hereditary, organic, and environmental factors, many, if
not most, are not. But parents often misperceive exploratory

behavior as "willful running." They fail to understand that
this period is a time when the child normally explores without an awareness of danger and therefore needs a specific
protective response. Although this parental misperception
may represent a projection of issues unresolved in one or
both parents, the child ultimately internalizes the parental
view of his behavior as willful running.

The next subphase, rapprochement, is a particularly
vulnerable one for the child and requires an especially
flexible response. During this phase (ages 15-25 months)
the child no longer leaves the mother without concern about
her whereabouts; curiosity alternates with anxiety about
being too far away from her. Behaviorally, the child clings
and demands one moment and returns to his explorations the
next. It is as if he suddenly becomes aware that he is not
as separate or autonomous as he had felt a moment before;
he needs his mother's physical presence and emotional support
and holding until his tenuous sense of autonomy is reestab-
lished. We know that during this time the child's evocative
memory capacity--the ability to remember a person even though
the person is not present and even though the child may be
angry at that person--is being established and is therefore
unstable (Fraiberg, 1969).

The important nurturing people in the child's world
must be flexible, empathic, and separate if they are to
respond to the rapidly changing needs of the child and not
project their own unresolved issues onto him. A depressed,
emotionally unavailable mother, or one whose availability is
inconsistent, cannot provide the appropriate responses
necessary for the child's successful achievement of object
constancy. The result may be the child's regression to and
fixation at the practicing subphase, with the specific
problems of either willful running or failure to achieve
object constancy, manifest by indiscriminate running to
various people for support. Another manifestation of regression to the practicing subphase may be seen in later years
in the rage that is a large component of impulsive acts.
In these instances the older child or adult reexperiences
early disappointment and reacts once again with the remembered rage of the early experience.

Some adults with serious character disorders in which
impulsivity is a major component have been included by Kern-

berg (1967, 1970, 1975) as persons with both borderline
personality organization and narcissistic personalities.
(For him, the latter group is composed of the better functioning antisocial personalities.) Kohut (1971) has described
similar impulsive patients as narcissistic personalities.
Several reasons may explain the use of both diagnostic labels
for these patients: (1) primitive, impulse-ridden patients
can be ranged along a continuum that includes borderline and
narcissistic personalities; their impulsivity can range from
an isolated act following a specific stress to a manifestation of chronic ego weakness; (2) different frameworks
generate different diagnostic categorizations: Kernberg's
framework emphasizes object relations theory while Kohut
focuses on self-esteem and the formation of the self; (3)
the treatment concepts and styles that emerge from Kernberg's
and Kohut's personality formulations may focus on and therefore elicit different personality aspects in similar or
overlapping groups of patients. Since the formulations of
both theorists have important treatment implications for
primitive, impulse-ridden patients, I will outline some pertinent aspects of their work.

Kernberg (1967, 1968, 1975) emphasizes the relatively
stable aspects of borderline patients and nonspecific signs
of ego weakness, including impulsivity, as well as the use of
primitive defenses, such as splitting, primitive idealization,
projection and projective identification, denial, omnipotence,
and devaluation. He stresses the concept of splitting, in
which the patient must separate positive from negative images,
feelings, and fantasies of a valued person in order to pre-
serve the person as an image. Kernberg's psychotherapeutic
approach with borderlines emphasizes the negative transfer-
ence--that is, the anger that emerges in these patients during treatment--as an important reflection of the anger in
their everyday lives. Since this anger can be very disruptive, he feels that it must be contained by structuring the
treatment and limit-setting. He also holds that the primitive defenses of these patients must be confronted to help
them look at their anger and envy. This confrontational,
interpretive approach is illustrated in many of Kernberg's
clinical vignettes in which his personal style may play a
role in eliciting the patient's anger.

Other observers (Adler, 1975a; Buie and Adler, 1972;
Masterson, 1975) have also confirmed anger as a major theme

in work with borderlines. It emerges when inevitable disappointments occur in therapy, especially since these patients idealize their therapists and cannot tolerate their
own feelings when their unrealistic expectations are not met.
At such times, their impulsivity may become manifest.

Kohut's definition of the narcissistic personality (1971)
centers on the two major types of transference that appear
in treatment, which he refers to as "mirror" and "idealizing."
In the mirror transference, the patient's grandiose aspects
are paramount as he relates to the therapist with different
degrees of merger or separation. The major function of the
therapist may be his acknowledgement or "mirroring", --
his appreciation of the words and productions of the patient.
It is during the emergence of the mirror transference that
acting out and impulsivity are most likely to occur, for it
is at this time that a breakthrough of the grandiose self
occurs, accompanied by a blurring of the distinction between
thought, feeling, and action. In the idealizing transference, the therapist is seen as the embodiment of all perfec-
tion, derived in part from the patients' projections of his
grandiosity onto the therapist.

According to Kohut, these two qualities of a person--
the grandiose and the idealizing--eventually merge, lead
gradually to the formation of a cohesive self, and are related
to the development of solid self-esteem. However, emergence
of these aspects in the transference are also evidence of
self-esteem vulnerability--indications that cohesive self-
formation has not been achieved--and he ascribes these vul-
nerabilities to major disappointments in idealized parental
figures. Such disappointments are obvious in the backgrounds
of primitive impulse-ridden patients. The grandiosity of
these patients, as well as their idealization of others and
the disappointments following these idealizations, are well
known. The magical, grandiose, unrealistic impulsivity of
the narcissistic personality can be contrasted with the
impulsivity associated with rage that appears more readily
in the borderline personality following feelings of abandonment and aloneness.

Kohut holds that a treatment approach that leads to
a process whereby missing ego and superego functions are
internalized has three basic dimensions: (1) it allows
mirroring and idealizing transferences to emerge; (2) it

empathically responds to and interprets the transference (as well as current and past disappointments); and (3) it offers frustration under optimal circumstances. This process, which he calls "transmuting internalization," slowly leads to "structure formation" in the patient. As self-regard functions increase within the person's ego and superego, decreased dependence on others, either to provide mirroring (appreciation) or to be available for idealization, occurs.

I feel that aspects of the formulations of such workers as Winnicott, Mahler, Kernberg, Kohut, as well as Balint (1968) and Guntrip (1971), can be integrated to provide a treatment framework for impulse-ridden patients in a variety of settings. Our treatment task is to conceptualize the ways that constructive outside experiences in the patient's current life can be internalized and become part of his personality. How can these patients who lack certain structures and functions develop them? What kinds of therapeutic experiences in what kinds of settings are necessary for a group of patients often felt to be among the most untreatable?

I believe that such concepts as the holding environment, good-enough mothering, and separation-individuation subphases and failures are directly applicable to these patients in any setting.

For example, we have learned that prisoners in a successful program are very sensitive to appropriate amounts of support and holding. This is evidenced by occasional requests from inmates for transfer from a medium to a maximum security prison; the fact that they are counted five times in the maximum security prison and only once in the other facility emerges as we explore their reasons. And, predictably, their histories often reveal backgrounds of neglect and abandonment in which parents were unaware of or did not care about the whereabouts of their young child.

For other inmates, aspects of separation-individuation issues can be seen in the details of arranging a work-release program. Here the availability of personnel who understand the inmate's wishes for autonomy and his simultaneous fear of separation and need for appropriate support is crucial. The tendency of inmates to run is often preceded by subtle warnings and hints. The staff sensitive to the pathological

reliving of "practicing subphase" failures and the need for
holding and control can ultimately help such people trust,
feel held, and put into words their confusing and conflicting dilemmas.

These issues are similar to those found in treating
borderline and narcissistic personality disorders, but
treatment of the impulsive person emphasizes the presenting
impulsivity as the avenue to initial engagement between patient and therapist. The implications of the treatment
models and methods of workers with borderlines and narcissistic personalities (Adler, 1974, 1975a, 1976; Buie and Adler,
1972; Kernberg, 1975; Kohut, 1971) are useful because they
can help translate developmental concepts into treatment
models with adult impulse-ridden patients in a variety of
settings. Therapeutic tasks would include allowing mirror
and idealizing transferences to flourish--with prison, clinic
or hospital staff--and the testing of verbalized anger
as something that does not destroy.

The first requirement for any treatment program, whether
in a therapist's private office or within an institutional
setting, is a careful diagnostic evaluation that provides
a detailed history. A formulation arising from this diagnostic material can include an understanding of the precipitating
stresses that face the individual, the level of his capacities for handling the stress, and the solutions he chooses
Ultimately the results of this formulation should be an
understanding that can define the specific failures of good-
enough mothering at specific developmental levels, and an
assessment of the nature of the holding environment responses
necessary for the individual patient.

The evaluation of the patient's strengths and weaknesses
helps determine not only the specific level of vulnerability
and need, but also the type of setting required. In a court
context, for example, this careful evaluation can form an
important part of the recommendation to the court about the
setting necessary for effective treatment. On the one hand,
individuals with relatively solid ego and superego development whose transient impulsivity is symptomatic of conflict
occurring under stress can often be treated in a private
office. On the other hand, those who have more acute prob-
lems--less capacity for control, greater destructive and
self-destructive potential, and family disorganization and/or

questionable family support--may require yet another type of
setting, such as a court clinic or court-ordered private
treatment. Finally, some patients require a holding environment that includes locks, such as a hospital or prison setting. Thus the holding environment I am defining is made
up of the quality of therapist-patient interaction as well
as its extension beyond the patient and therapist into the
external environment as evaluation deems necessary.

The impulse-ridden patient often tests the therapist's
or the environment's capacity to establish the appropriate
holding environment for him. Years of distrust, projection,
running, and impulsivity must inevitably emerge and be experienced before the new environment can begin to be trusted
and feel safe. The therapist's and staff's capacity to en-
dure, understand, and explore this testing, which is often
very provocative, can be a major achievement and often requires all the skill and empathic capacity of everyone involved.

The countertransference feelings that the more primitive
impulse-ridden patients provoke in therapist and staff are
manifold and powerful. They include murderous rage, a wish
to reject the patient or to retaliate and punish, withdrawal,
hopelessness and helplessness, and viewing the patient as
totally bad, manipulative, and undeserving of treatment (Adler, 1970, 1972, 1975a, b; Adler and Buie, 1972). It is the
manifestation of these countertransference feelings within
society that impedes application of our knowledge, and it is
necessary to emphasize them here, if only briefly.

The anger and projections of impulse-ridden people are
felt and responded to frequently in a punitive, rejecting,
angry way. The feeling often consists of the wish to extrude
and rid oneself of such "evil," dangerous people. Although
the therapist's countertransference feelings are responses
to a patient, they are nonetheless feelings that belong to
the person experiencing them. If these countertransference
feelings consist of a fury and a wish to destroy, it is
understandable that such feelings would be consciously unacceptable to the person having them--and something that he
would want to repudiate. When this psychodynamic mechanism
is applied to society, it follows that people who represent
exaggerated forms of unacceptable fury would be rejected and
expelled because this heightened fury is present in latent

form in the society. This formulation helps explain why
prisons are built far away from areas of high population
density.

In addition, the difficulties of impulse-ridden persons
elicit few empathic responses, and their needs are low on
the social planning hierarchy. The negative responses to
attempts to develop community-based treatment facilities
illustrate this phenomenon. Perhaps correctional systems
that are separated from parole systems, which are in turn
separated from probation systems (in many states), are more
than merely self-perpetuating bureaucratic structures. In
part they represent society's rejection of this population by
failing to develop a continuous, supportive holding environment for them (Adler, 1975b).

Failures of empathy are also evident in society's failure to provide adequate compensatory structures in the
schools, social agencies, courts, and prisons. The opportunity for a continuous holding environment, which could
be achieved through the utilization of one supportive therapeutic figure with limit-setting capabilities for a patient
and/or family over a long period of time, is rarely available
in practice. Instead, we more often see a fragmentation of
services and functions that reinforces the tendency toward
fragmentation in these impulsive individuals and their
families.

To return to treatment issues: if the holding environment established through adequate reality structuring and
empathic therapist responses is correctly formulated and
applied, the patient ultimately feels safe and held. The
inmate referred to earlier who would shoot anyone dumb enough
to stand in his way during an armed robbery provides an example. His early stance in treatment was one of aloofness and
indifference, and he required a specific, empathic approach
and confrontation for successful engagement.

When he missed his third appointment, his therapist
wrote him a note stating that he would expect to see him
the following week. During the next session, the patient explained that he had tried out for the baseball
team at the time of his last appointment. The therapist's repeated statement, "But I was here waiting for
you," which followed every rationalization by the patient

for the missed appointment, led to the patient's uncontrolled weeping. The story which emerged revealed
that the patient's aloofness covered over a painful
loneliness and longing for a mother who had repeatedly
disappointed him. The therapist's confrontation permitted the beginning of a trusting relationship in which
patient and therapist could explore these disappointments. This aloof patient in this supportive setting
became a profoundly depressed man who felt overwhelming
guilt for his antisocial actions of the past and his
increasing awareness of his anger at his formerly
idealized mother.

Ultimately, however, this inmate began to develop solid
self-esteem, after several years of predominantly alter-
nating mirror and idealizing transferences. Coincident
with the improved self-esteem, he showed evidence of
identifying with aspects of his therapist's role. While
in the prison he volunteered to meet with groups of pre-
delinquents as a way of helping them learn about the
expected consequences of their current actions. His
talented style in relating to them gave him much satisfaction and led to his work after leaving prison as
counselor of impulsive persons.

Although not detailed in the foregoing example, the therapist must anticipate that the patient will both welcome and
fear the implications of the safe holding environment--an environment from which he may have been running for years. Depending on the specific patient, emergent fears include mutual
destruction, merger, or loss of autonomy. The empathic understanding of these issues can lead to their exploration in
the treatment setting.

Although I stress a therapist-patient approach, I feel
that these formulations can be applied to a larger framework,
such as a hospital ward or prison setting. An important
observation in prisons, which offer little that might be
called therapeutic, is that a certain percentage of inmates
do mature significantly and remain out of prison after
release. In interviewing some of these former inmates, I
have been impressed by the fact that almost all have found
someone--a fellow inmate with certain specific strengths,
a shop foreman, or an officer--whom the inmate described as
particularly important to him during the time that coincided

with his growth. This new and valued person seemed to possess varying combinations of the ability to mirror, or be idealized, and/or tolerate the provocations and rage of the inmate. I am suggesting that we can understand these significant relationships within the framework I have presented, and can build them more deliberately into a treatment setting rather than encountering them as relatively infrequent occurrences.

Whether the specific response required by the patient is mirroring, allowing idealization, or tolerating fury, the empathic understanding of these needs, and the appropriate response to them (including clarification and interpretation), can ultimately lead to an internalization process in the patient. We still have much to learn about this process, the ways to facilitate its occurrence, and the vigilance to countertransference responses that impede it. But there is sufficient evidence of such internalization processes occurring in impulse-ridden people to engender hope that as our knowledge increases, we can apply what we know with greater effect.

References

Adler, G. 1970. Valuing and devaluing in the psychotherapeutic process. Arch. Gen. Psychiatry, 22, 454-461.

Adler, G. 1972. Helplessness in the helpers. Br. J. Med. Psychol., 45, 315-326.

Adler, G. 1974. Regression in psychotherapy: Disruptive or therapeutic? Int. J. Psychoan. Psychother., 4, 252-264.

Adler, G. 1975a. The usefulness of the "borderline" concept in psychotherapy. In J.E. Mack (Ed.), Borderline States in Psychiatry. New York: Grune & Stratton.

Adler, G. 1975b. Correctional (prison) psychiatry. In A.M. Freedman, H.I. Kaplan, and B.J. Sadock (Eds.), Comprehensive Textbook of Psychiatry. Second Edition. Baltimore: Williams & Wilkins, 2437-2442.

Adler, G. and Buie, D.H., Jr. 1972. The misuses of confrontation with borderline patients. Int. J. Psychoanal. Psychother., 1, 109-120.

Adler, G. and Buie, D.H., Jr. 1976. The process of psy-
    chotherapy in the treatment of borderline patients.
    Presented at the Eleventh Tufts Symposium on Psychother-
    apy, Boston, Mass.
Aichhorn, A. Wayward Youth. 1935. New York: Viking Press
Balint, M. 1968. The Basic Fault: Therapeutic Aspects of
    Regression. London: Tavistock Publications.
Bernabeau, E.P. 1958. Underlying ego mechanisms in de-
    linquency. Psychoanal. Q., 27, 383-396.
Buie, D.H., Jr. and Adler, G. 1972. The uses of confron-
    tation with borderline patients. Int. J. Psychoanal.
    Psychother., 90-108.
Fraiberg, S. 1969. Libidinal object constancy and mental
    representation. The Psychoanalytic Study of the Child,
    Vol. 24, 9-47. New York: International Universities
    Press.
Guntrip. H. 1971. Psychoanalytic Theory, Therapy, and the
    Self. New York: Basic Books.
Hartmann, H. 1958. Ego Psychology and the Problem of Adapta-
    tion. New York: International Universities Press.
Kernberg, O.F. 1967. Borderline personality organization.
    J. Am. Psychoanal. Assoc., 15, 641-685.
Kernberg, O.F. 1968. The treatment of patients with bor-
    derline personality organization. Int. J. of Psycho-
    anal., 49, 600-619.
Kernberg, O.F. 1970. Factors in the psychoanalytic treat-
    ment of narcissistic personalities. J. Am. Psychoanal.
    Assoc., 18, 51-85.
Kernberg, O.F. 1975. Borderline Conditions and Pathologi-
    cal Narcissism. New York: Jason Aronson.
Kohut, H. 1971. The Analysis of the Self. New York:
    International Universities Press.
Mahler, M.S. 1971. A study of the separation-individuation
    process and its possible relevance to borderline phenome-
    na in the psychoanalytic situation. The Psychoanalytic
    Study of the Child. Vol. 26, 403-424. New York: Inter-
    national Universities Press.
Mahler, M.S. 1972. Rapprochement subphase of the separa-
    tion-individuation process. Psychoanal. Q., 41, 487-
    506.
Masterson, J.E. 1976. Psychotherapy of the Borderline
    Adult: A Developmental Approach. New York: Brunner/
    Mazel.
Robins, L.N. 1966. Deviant Children Grown Up: A Sociologi-
    cal and Psychiatric Study of Sociopathic Personality.
    Baltimore: Williams & Wilkins.

Semrad, E.V. 1969. Teaching Psychotherapy of Psychotic
    Patients. New York: Grune & Stratton.
Winnicott, D.W. 1965. The Maturational Processes and the
    Facilitating Environment. New York: International
    Universities Press.

DETERMINANTS OF IMPULSIVE BEHAVIOR: TOWARD AN INTEGRATION

OF SOCIAL AND PSYCHOLOGICAL FACTORS

Norman E. Zinberg, M.D.

Associate Clinical Professor of Psychiatry, Har-
vard Medical School, and Psychiatrist-in-Chief,
Washingtonian Center for Addictions, Boston,
Massachusetts

This paper will be concerned not so much with the clinical aspects of extreme and serious destructive acts, but with
a group of "middle-range" behaviors commonly referred to as
impulse disorders. Rather than focusing on those individuals
in jails or mental hospitals who might be overwhelmingly
violent, the group I will be concerned with comprises those
persons who may be sufficiently concerned about their behavior to become outpatients, as well as those who do not
become patients at all. This group does not have the terri-
fyingly disturbed childhoods described in many cases; they
have not been badly abused, or beaten, or sexually assaulted,
and so forth. But they comprise a population often labeled
"impulse disorder" because of a sexual preoccupation, drug
use, or any one of a number of socially disapproved practices. Often a variety of pejorative words, such as "psychopath" and "sociopath," are too loosely used to describe
these individuals, with the implication that their ego control mechanisms are weak.

Some writers describe persons with "impulse disorders"
as almost literally lacking ego controls available to other
people--as if controls are nonexistent, due either to congenital defect or because the problem developed so early in
life that it could be viewed, at least in function, as a
congenital defect. As a therapist I often have difficulty

19

differentiating (theoretically and technically, not literally) between congenital problems and those assumed to have
become fixed during the first year or two of life. The latter are seen as developing so early that, to me, they seem to
be descriptions of congenital defects. In discussions of
impulse disorders the superego is often viewed in a similar
fashion--as a "given," almost congenital in nature; it is
either weak and ineffective or full of lacunae. At the same
time, however, it is viewed as completely punishing, with
little potential for either a reasonable range of guilt or
for being very useful to the individual in the aid of self-
control.

These "impulse" matters are approached in two ways. One
is through the observable behavior itself; people are often
labeled "impulse disorders" because they have done something
considered "bad." Murderers are often legitimately placed
in this category because they murdered, and I would like to
exempt them from my discussion because practically no known
society has found murder an acceptable behavior. But if we
consider con men, promiscuous individuals, drug users, homo-
sexuals--a series of persons engaging in what might be considered perversions--this group is labeled as having "impulse disorders" almost solely on society's definition of the
acceptability of that behavior.

The second category of individuals labeled impulse
disorders are those who describe an intense, often overwhelming feeling in themselves--almost an uncontrollable urge--
which is at least in part acted upon. In my clinical experience I have never seen a person with a so-called impulse
disorder who always acted on the impulse: at times the
impulse would be acted upon; at other times, not. These
persons would not, then, be at all totally disordered, although they are often treated or looked upon as if they were.
They are described as having enormous difficulties in delay-
ing gratification. Although this description can be applied
to homosexuality and drug abuse, it can also include such
matters as eating too much chocolate cake or too many potato
chips, or smoking cigarettes. I even recall a patient who
was impelled to ride the right airplane. He had a preoccupation with machinery and felt that if he could not get on
the right airplane he would suffer enormously; he had consequently been labeled by a psychiatrist as having an impulse disorder.

Once someone is labeled "impulse disorder," the therapeutic emphasis focuses on the issue of control--that is,
stopping the "bad" behavior--rather than on making careful
distinctions between when a person can deal with the impulse
and when he cannot. The attempt to recognize when a person
is inhibited from using available ego controls, and is thereby
making infrequent use of them, is far different from imagining that he literally lacks such controls.

Those people who choose acceptable impulses, even if
they are very difficult to control, are less likely to be
categorized as "impulse disorders." They are more likely
to be described as narcissistic personalities who are very
involved with private concerns. In contrast, those involved
in illegal activities (which result in public concern) are
seen as impulse disorders, regardless of the degree of control. Often the manifestations of their illegal impulses
are described in terms approaching that of psychotic behavior; people cannot understand why else they would take such
terrible risks. Thus the concept of impulse disorder rests,
to a large extent, on the degree to which the behavior is
socially unacceptable because, as we know, the behavior is
often acceptable to the individual on a conscious level.
In other words, many persons with impulse disorders say to
all of us: "I really want to do this, and I don't think
it's so bad. But I run into a terrible conflict because
everybody else thinks it's so awful."

At this point, it seems to me, we find an enormous amount
of cultural relativism, and I want to cite a recent Danish
study in this regard (Kutchinsky, 1976). Denmark may be a
very repressed culture because a great deal of voyeurism
occurs; the number of cases, according to figures, seems to
be enormous--the reasons for which I have no understanding.
In an effort to rectify the situation, the government changed
the laws and made peepshows and other similar activities
legal. As many aspects of voyeurism as possible were le-
gitimized and therefore available to people who wanted to
use them. And lo and behold, the incidence of voyeurism in
Denmark dropped to virtually nothing. Kutchinsky's study
was a long-term followup of people who had previously been
voyeurs and who attended peepshows. Indeed, many of the
people who went to peepshows were formerly voyeurs. With
legalization, however, they were no longer regarded as criminals, and in fact were no longer categorized as having im-

pulse disorders. They reported they could delay gratification as long as they knew the means for gratification would
be legitimately available to them when they wanted it.
Thus, simply by legitimizing both the behavior that had been
socially unacceptable and the means for its gratification,
large numbers of impulse disorders were "cured." Many of
these "patients" were not disturbed in any other area but
voyeurism. But because their voyeurism and its control had
become such a major factor in their lives, they used more and
more of their energy trying to protect themselves against
both their voyeuristic impulses and dealing with the social
consequences of those impulses. The followup study shows all
this to have virtually disappeared.

We do not have to look far to see that an active social
dimension operated in the behavior of these voyeurs, and we
must wonder whether or not this same extremely important
social factor operates in many of what we term impulse disorders. My clinical experience in recent years in this
country has provided many instances that correspond closely
to the Danish phenomenon. A phrase often heard, and one
that has become one of my least favorite phrases in all
psychiatry--"acting out"--may well be losing its currency.
The term has been long estranged from its original meaning
of specific activities related directly to the transference,
and has been used too often to indicate anything the authority
employing it might disapprove of. For example, promiscuous
behavior that in the fifties would have been seen as "acting
out," and regarded by many people as an impulse disorder, is
now often regarded as reasonable sexual experimentation.

The greatest change that I have seen in the last few
years in this country is in the area of homosexuality.
What we are witnessing is similar to what occurred regarding
voyeurism in Denmark. The trend of openness and increasing
acceptance of homosexuality in many areas of society appears
to have reduced enormously the subvert behavior instanced,
for example, by persons loitering around the toilets in subway
stations--a degrading way of making contact that was a very
prominent and painful phenomenon in the fifties.

In the past, many homosexuals had been labeled by psychiatrists as impulse disorders. However, while homosexual de-
dire may be strongly held, it is now far less likely to be
seen or to be experienced as an overriding impulse. Rather,
it has come bo be viewed as far more similar to heterosexual

practices, and while nonconformist, would not in and of itself classify an individual as having an impulse-ridden
character disorder. Going to a prostitute, in this culture,
would be another example of behavior that has lost considerable social disapprobation.

In my own particular area of interest, controlled heroin
use, I begin to see a very similar phenomenon. For whatever
reasons, heroin is beginning to be viewed as something whose
use can be controlled and is not, per se, the overwhelming,
addictive substance it had been thought to be; more people
seem to be able to control its use. In fact, the case could
be made that with the growing acceptance of modes of controlling use, the pressures have been reduced. Although some
types of personality structures truly cannot deal with impulses, I think that in these cases the problems stem from
psychological blocks and inhibitions rather than absence of
the potential for control. In my view, a heroin user does
not lack controls. Rather, his wish for certain satisfactions,
such as to see himself as weak, outweighs and blocks his
wishes for control.

With regard to how behavior becomes acceptable in our
society, I hold that the majority of the population constantly
integrates the inchoate messages received from the media,
peer groups, parental responses, and institutional statements
(laws, legal changes, school rules, etc.,) with their own
cultural attitudes and precepts. The process of integrating
these responses involves a crucial dimension: weighing and
assessing the extent and availability of knowledge and social
supports surrounding a particular sort of behavior. This
entire process, in all its complexity, defines the extent
of the risk involved. While there are those at one end of
the continuum within the general population who will take
no risks at all, there are others who look for chances and
adventures. And the extent to which their interest in ad-
venture moves to a destructive extreme depends on their capacity to make use of social supports.

For example, people who began to use marihuana in 1964
were quite different from those who used marihuana in the
1940s or in the 1920s. Those in the more recent group were
clearly experimenters and risk-takers, but not necessarily
to the same extent as those who had become involved in the
same situation twenty and forty years earlier. During earlier

times these individuals comprised a small, isolated social
group--bohemians. Marihuana users who began in 1964,
before usage was socially acceptable, in turn appear considerably more like people with a stake in provoking or ex-
posing the straight culture than did those who began use in
1969. And by 1975 in some parts of California, 20-year-old
nonusers who decided not to try marihuana could have been
called upon to explain themselves because their behavior was
statistically outside the realm of usual behavior. In a
Sausalito high school, for example, where 80 percent of the
students were marihuana users, the 20 percent who were nonusers were, ironically, the deviants.

I participated in a study concluded in 1975 in which a
panel of "experts" was enlisted to study in-depth interviews
that had been conducted throughout the country in a study of
youthful behavior. Our task was to extract material from
cases and interviews indicating what made drug-taking risky
in terms of potential psychological trouble for individuals.
Without exception, the five psychiatrists who were members
of the panel, after reading a number of the interviews,
clearly labeled some of the nondrug users as more at risk
than the great majority of the drug users. This obviously
did not include those nondrug users who did not use because
their interests were genuinely elsewhere, but did include
those whose self-righteousness about the issue seemed to mask
a genuine insecurity concerning their capacity to handle any
untoward experience. Again, at one end of the scale of drug
users, some could be labeled at risk, in that they were
not making use of certain controls and were at war with
society in some regard or other. But the great majority of
the drug users were seen as more normative than some nonusers, some could be labeled at risk, in that they were
tle, puritanical, and excessively concerned with being good,
their fear of loss of control placed them more at psychological risk than those in the user group.

Whether this information sheds more light on psychiatrists' perceptions than on cultural change is difficult to
know. But if the study had been done ten years earlier,
judging from changes that have occurred in my own attitudes
toward many contemporary phenomena, I think assessments concerning persons at risk would have been very different.
During those ten years a great deal of social learning had
taken place, and the overall view of what was occurring had
changed.

Generally speaking, psychoanalytic theory has paid the greatest amount of attention regarding basic impulses to influences on the development of what we call the ego--identity--and its relationship to these basic impulses, particularly in the earliest developmental phases. In object relations theory, which focused most strongly on these relationships, the early capacities to take objects in and then to make those objects part of the self are viewed as being closely connected to the notion of primitive drives or impulses. I do not believe the fundamental issue concerning ego development is whether these drives or impulses are biologically rooted or whether they are derived from mode of separation from the mother in the earliest years. Too little coherent and consistent attention has been paid to what is taken in ("introjected") from the outside--the social milieu, the social setting--and how this affects personality development over time.

In assessing the ego capacities of drug users, for example, I find that their behavior has been influenced to an important degree by social changes and social learning during the past ten to fifteen years. An example of this social learning can be seen by comparing the experiences of people who took LSD in 1963 with those who took it in 1973. In 1963, people believed they could experience heaven or hell from the drug--from attaining mystical oneness, spiritual rebirth, or great insight, to going crazy (that is, really going over the edge). And indeed, many did go over the edge at that time, although those who used LSD earlier did not, and people who used it later did not. During the time, however, when the culture believed in the drug's extraordinary effects, those effects actually occurred. I therefore feel that the social setting, as much as the personality of the user of the drug, was implicated in what happened.

Actual descriptions of the experiences are of special interest. In 1963, because of the anxiety aroused by use of the drug, people generally reported very remarkable experiences; they really felt that they had been shocked by what they had experienced, that breakthroughs occurred at all levels of their personality structure, that they had sustained experiences both enormously interesting and enormously frightening. In 1973, after ten years of understanding these drug reactions--that is, after a great deal of experience throughout the culture, during which changes in music, colors, designs, etc.

had been reported--different sorts of reports appeared.
People could take a tab of LSD, look around, and say: "Oh,
that's what a psychedelic color is like; that's what it feels
like to 'trip'; that's what they've been talking about."
In other words, the social learning that had taken place in
that ten-year period--the extent of the integration of many
notions, ideas, or knowledge--had resulted in a change in
the experience itself: users' ego structures began to dis-
count the drug's powerful aspects.

I think this decline in reacting to the drug as a powerful agent has very little to do with the personality of the
user. As a result of the experience of the social milieu
and its expectations, the drug experience itself was different. It became almost exclusively a secondary process
experience, and a great deal of evidence exists to support
this. The drug-user population I have been studying is often
referred to as "impulse disordered"--a judgment made on a
purely psychological basis. The results of our research,
however, indicate that social changes have been an important
determinant in the behavior of these individuals.

Another similar type of research with which I have been
involved concerns giving THC (tetrahydrocannabinol--the active
ingredient in marihuana) and marihuana to people who have
been receiving cancer chemotherapy at a cancer center in
Boston. With regard to reactions to the drug, we have found
three distinct groups of people: those who are marihuana-
experienced; those who are marihuana-naive but know a lot
about the drug (their friends have used it, their children
have used it, and they have an idea of what it is all about);
and those who are truly marihuana-naive. Most of those in
the latter group are elderly people, but we have tried to
correct for age in our understanding of their reactions.
All dysphoric reactions come from the third group. While
the reactions of the first two groups were fairly consistent,
the elderly occasionally become dysphoric, highly sedated,
or euphoric, and have a lot of difficulty understanding what
is happening to them.

My contention is that as the environment changes, and
as people must deal with social change--that is, specific
demands from a variety of environmental sources--certain of
their capacities to deal with this environment also change.
And as people begin to deal with the environment differently,

how they deal with other aspects of their behavior also
changes. The young woman who was extremely sexually inhibited early in the 1950s but in the early 1970s experienced
a great deal of sexual activity may still be expressing,
somewhere deep down, exactly the same internal conflict.
She may therefore be no more and no less "impulse ridden"
than she was before; she may only have decided on a different solution to very much the same problem. However, pursuant
to her changed behavior, other changes also occur: people
see her differently, she sees herself differently, and her
reactions and choices based on these new perceptions may
provide her with behavioral changes in other aspects of
her life.

Ronald Laing has always been interested in very primitive
experiences (with varying emphases throughout his career).
In one of his poems in Knots (1970), he says: "Jack wants
Jill to love him / so he tells her he loves her. / Jill wants
Jack to love her / so she tells him she loves him. / They
have a relationship." Laing in his pithy way is trying to
indicate the dynamics of a narcissistic disorder. But I
often want to know what happens during this relationship,
regardless of its narcissistic basis, when Jack and Jill
begin to see themselves as two interacting people--a couple.
What occurs as a result of the changes wrought by this social
fact? In analogous fashion, a crucial question regarding
what we label as "impulse disorders" would be: What occurs
as impulse metamorphosis and change take place consequent to
social attitude change toward particular acts previously
called "impulsive"?

To an important extent, what we refer to as impulse
disorders are actually one more psychological expression of
the moral values of the reigning culture, which are constantly changing. This is not to say that the girl who was inhibited at one time and is promiscuous at another does not
have some emotional difficulty and sexual conflict that
inhibits her self-awareness and limits her pleasurable expression of feeling. Her conflict may be just as real in one
case as in the other. However, impulse disorders have been
seen principally as extremely primitive problems, based
almost exclusively on very early developmental defects or
arrests. Very little attention has been given to the fact
that the impulses generally seen as problematic are socially
unacceptable and are viewed as deviant by the individual and

by the reigning cultural outlook. As a result of this view
of deviance and the unacceptable nature of certain wishes,
my contention is that these wishes attain greater prominence,
often from a very early time in the life of the individual,
than if they had not been normatively defined as deviant.
They then become readily connected in large degree to the
struggle with the reigning social norms.

Kai Erikson (1966) presents a particular theory of
deviance, often employed by social anthropologists, in a
very compelling way. He maintains that deviance--and he
uses words that are very close to the concept of impulse--
has as important a function within the society as nondeviance
does. Society at large in fact attempts to define its own
limits by requiring that some people be deviant. The majority
can in this way define what is appropriate and acceptable at
a particular historical moment.

Acts of violence seem to many to be closer to representing true impulse disorders, but I am not at all sure that
even these acts are entirely impulse disorders. The ways
in which violence is expressed at the moment may well be an
impulse disorder of our time. Have we unleashed, or has
society asked for, certain ways to express underlying issues?
With all the suggestions for abolishing or decreasing violence on television, the facts are that these are the most
popular programs throughout the viewing public. Their popularity indicates that an important chord is being sounded
in the hearts and minds of the populace, and it is not likely
to be understood or dealt with by simply reducing the number of programs containing violence. I do not mean by this
to support violence on TV. But I do mean to emphasize that
the popularity of this violence is cause for serious con-
sideration--by citizens, behavioral scientists, policymakers.
At the present time, however, rather than focusing on why
these programs are so popular, efforts are almost solely
concerned with stopping them.

The struggle with the cultural or social norms is potentially shared or engaged in by all. Each of us deals with
such issues, and one can speculate about why one person gets
attached to a culturally unacceptable wish and another person does not. I think that attachment to such a wish does
come from very early, very primitive preoccupations in certain family structures. But because I also think that most of

us face these issues at one time or another, I note that at certain times we resolve them in one way, and at other times, another. And the chosen direction depends on cultural expectations as well as individual life experience at that particular time. In this regard I think Erik Erikson's idea that at different historical periods there are different solutions to the same problem is certainly very cogent (1950). But the basic issues are always with us in one way or another because the problem of living within one's skin--solving separation/individuation issues, achieving independence, sexual or otherwise--presents complexities for everyone. The likelihood that a certain percentage of people will find it difficult to work them through seems to be very great.

Unacceptable wishes are connected to a variety of other issues. The potential for the control of such wishes becomes less possible as societal sanctions against them become more stringent. The individual becomes estranged from what he had formerly used as control measures because the relation between what his psyche and what society sanctions becomes confused. In order for him to maintain operative controls over the rest of his structure, he often compartmentalizes the unacceptable impulse.

In my clinical work I find this process of crucial significance. As these impulses, considered illicit or illegal, become compartmentalized--separated off--they are not allowed to work their way through all the aspects of the ego structure. This psychological removal from more usual and effective control mechanisms occurs after the impulses have begun to be considered unacceptable--first by the society, then by the individual. The individual then struggles both with himself and with society and becomes increasingly involved with separating the impulse from the rest of his emotional life. Through this process he leaves the impulses to the superego for mastery (or control). But the superego is incapable of handling such tasks when ego controls are unavailable. Their availability depends on an equilibrated relation between impulse satisfaction and socially defined notions of appropriateness. In the situation just described, the necessary equilibrium has been lost.

During periods of social transition, when previously unacceptable behavior is no longer unacceptable, people often rely on the superego for sanction. It is at these disjunc-

tive times--when the sanctioning forces of society and those
of the superego are out of phase--that behavior characterized
as impulse disorders are most likely to be in evidence.

References

B. Kutchinsky, 1976. Deviance and criminality: The case
     of the voyeur in a peeper's paradise. Dis. Nerv. Syst.,
     37: 145-151.
R.D. Laing, 1970. Knots. New York: Pantheon Books.
K. Erikson, 1966. The Wayward Puritan. New York: John
     Wiley.
E.H. Erikson, 1950. Childhood and Society. New York: Nor-
     ton.

ETIOLOGICAL ISSUES IN THE DEVELOPMENT OF SOCIOPATHS, CRIMINALS, AND IMPULSIVE PERSONALITIES

George E. Vaillant, M.D.

Professor of Psychiatry, Harvard Medical School
at The Cambridge Hospital, Cambridge, Massachusetts

A recent clipping in a Boston newspaper cited a sociological study suggesting that "peer group influences determine whether a specific youth will become delinquent. Sex,
race, social class, a broken home, or inner-city living have
relatively little influence." The study defined delinquency
in terms of the 40 percent of youths who have admitted keeping stolen goods and the 50 percent who admitted shoplift-
ing. In the face of such a nonspecific definition, I won-
dered how these social scientists would regard the patient
about whom I had been consulted that morning. This teenage
child of two alcoholic parents had in the previous six months
stabbed his teacher, pushed a brother out of a third-story
window, and been sent to jail for six years for manslaughter.
Had he simply fallen in with bad companions?

Analogous to research breakthroughs in schizophrenia,
advances in our understanding of the chronically impulsive
personality can only be achieved by rigorous systematic
investigation that excludes as well as includes closely examined factors, and by sophisticated assessment of the interaction between nature and nurture. If this procedure is
followed, we discover that sociological studies which have
emphasized slum environment and peer pressure, as well as
psychiatric studies which have emphasized overprotective
mothers and broken homes per se, have oversimplified the
problem. This paper will present three model etiological
studies that summarize the current state of the art. Unlike

31

most of the etiological literature in delinquency, all three
have a longitudinal perspective.

No one study is sufficient by itself; the problem of
sustained impulsive behavior is too complex. It is necessary to control for or exclude many variables in order to
bring others into proper perspective. In this paper I shall
focus on studies by Hutchings and Mednick (1976), Sheldon
and Eleanor Glueck (1950, 1968), and Lee Robins (1966) which
illustrate, respectively, the etiological importance of
genetic predisposition, gross neglect before five, and the
effect of a sociopathic and/or alcoholic father. When these
three independent variables are considered, the more popular etiological variables like birth injuries, encephalitis,
peer pressures, corruption through imprisonment, social class,
parental death, foster homes, slum residence, and maternal
overprotection can be shown to exert little independent
effect upon delinquency.

Using carefully matched controls, each of these studies
cited supplies a piece of the etiological puzzle. Admitted-
ly, each study suffers certain lacks and constraints but,
taken together, the studies suggest that the impulsive personality and future delinquent can be identified long before
he enters the courts. In order to distinguish nature from
nurture, the first study, by Hutchings and Mednick and coworkers, used the Danish centralized adoption, police, and
psychiatric registers. In so doing, their foci necessarily
excluded many diagnostic and environmental issues. The
second study, the Gluecks' (1950) fifteen-year prospective
follow-up of 500 children remanded to reform school, contrasted them with 500 controls matched for ethnic background,
intellectual ability, and type of residence. The Gluecks'
study offers the advantage of prospectively studied home
environments, and includes a systematic study of the mothers'
families. It also has the advantage of controlling for eth-
nicity, and equally important, it is, to my knowledge, the
only etiological study of delinquency that has been prospectively validated. The Gluecks' study suffers from lack of
multivariate data analysis and from focusing only on reform
school residents--a sampling procedure that exaggerates the
association of deleterious family environment with sustained
impulsive behavior. The study has no females, no blacks, and
minor delinquents were excluded from both control and experimental groups.

The third study, by Lee Robins (1966), represents a thirty-year retrospective follow-up of 524 referrals to a St. Louis child guidance clinic—two-thirds of whom were sent there for antisocial behavior. The Robins study has the advantages of including women, utilizing a more sophisticated design and data analysis, and employing more thorough psychiatric diagnosis and evaluation of follow-up subjects than the Gluecks' study; it also includes a more representative sample of antisocial children. Because of its retrospective design, however, the Robins research lacks accurate information on the mothers. Since the mother brought the child to the clinic, and since the relation between female alcoholism and delinquency is less easily identified in public records, maternal problems were seldom admitted or identified. The Robins study lacks prospective design and only sampled children referred to a child guidance clinic; it may thus have excluded children of families too disorganized to follow through with such a referral.

In reviewing the three studies, let me begin by comparing their three different definitions and criteria for impulsive persons: "criminals," "delinquents," and "sociopaths," respectively. Hutchings' and Mednick's definition of the term criminal was simply that the subject have appeared in the Danish central police register and have been convicted once of a major criminal offense. (Offenses like begging, traffic violations, and disorderly conduct were excluded.)

The Gluecks' criteria for use of the term delinquent was that the subject have been sent to a juvenile reformatory. This proved to be a more specific and meaningful criterion than might initially be expected. When the Gluecks compared their delinquents to socioeconomically matched controls, they found that not only did the two groups remain very different for fifteen years, but also that they had been very different in the years prior to reform school. Roughly half of the delinquents had been truant before age 10; roughly half had engaged in persistent misbehavior before 10. By junior high school, 59 percent had run away from home, 29 percent had begun using alcohol, and 62 percent were persistently truant. Each of these behavior variables was found in less than 2 percent of the matched controls. At the time of their first sentencing, 95 percent of the delinquents, but only 17 percent of the controls, had engaged in persis-

tent misbehavior in school: it is repetition not unique-
ness of deviant behavior that identifies the impulsive
personality.

The differences between the two groups proved stable
over time (Glueck and Glueck, 1968). Ninety-eight percent
of the delinquent sample were in jail at least once after age
17, and 60 percent were in jail on at least three different
occasions. Only 9 percent of the controls spent time in
jail, and this was usually for alcohol-related offenses.
Despite poverty, minority membership, and residence in high-
crime neighborhoods, by age 45 only 3 of the 500 controls
had serious criminal records unexplained by concomitant alcoholism. In contrast, between 12 and 25--50 percent of the
delinquent group--spent half of their lives in jail. This
chronic incarceration did not result from long sentences;
rather, it reflected the fact that between the ages of 12
and 25 the delinquent group averaged one arrest per year.

Other differences were evident between the socioeconomically matched controls and delinquents that are characteristic of impulsive personalities. Although carefully matched
for intelligence, the delinquent youths had tremendous difficulty in working or enjoying working. Thus six times as
many delinquents (60 percent) markedly disliked school.
Twice as many tested at 30 percent below their age level in
mathematical achievement, were classified as subnormal on
their military intelligence tests, and were classified by
their schools as mentally retarded and placed in special
classes. Only one fourth as many played competitive sports.
As adults, three times as many of the delinquents were on
public welfare and twice as many (62 percent) suffered significant unemployment after age 25. Not surprisingly, life
was far more dangerous for the delinquent group. In childhood, three times as many were run over by automobiles. By
age 32, twice as many delinquents as controls had died; death
by violence accounted for the difference.

Lee Robins has, I think, provided us with the best
research conceptualization of the impulsive personality, or
what she and the DSM II call "sociopathic personality."
Her criteria eschew abstract adjectives like impulsive and
depend upon the sheer repetitiveness of deviant behavior.
They thus transcend those class and sexual biases that allow
poor impulsive adolescents and men to go to jail and be

labeled criminals while permitting rich, impulsive adolescents
and women to go to mental hospitals and be labeled "borderlines." Within her framework, Robins asks that at least
five out of nineteen criteria be present; and in her study
she found that in fact eleven of the nineteen criteria were
present in the average sociopath (1966).

How did the 84 male child guidance clinic referrals
later labeled sociopaths compare with the 300-odd male clinic
referrals not so diagnosed? As adults the sociopaths were
five times as likely to have been vagrant or impulsive, to
use aliases, to die by violence, or to manifest severe marital difficulties. They were four times as likely to have had
a poor work history, multiple arrests, and to have been sexually promiscuous. They were three times as likely to have
been financially dependent, belligerent, and truant. They
were three times as likely to have exhibited a lack of guilt
and to have engaged in excessive drinking and pathological
lying. They were statistically more likely to have had multiple suicide attempts, polydrug abuse, and somatic complaints.

Turning from conceptualization to results, what evidence
did Hutchings and Mednick (1976) find that heredity is important in impulse disorder? They studied 1,145 adoptees--
all of them adopted Danish males born between 1927 and 1941--
who were between the ages of 30 and 44 at the time of follow-
up. They compared these adoptees with a similar number of
controls, matched by age, father's occupation, and residence,
and found that 16 percent of the adoptees, but only 9 percent of the controls, had criminal records. This raised the
question: Does the trauma of adoption lead to criminal
behavior? Hutchings and Mednick, therefore, examined the
criminal records of the fathers; 31 percent of the biological fathers of the adoptees, but only 13 percent of the adoptive fathers had criminal records. The incidence of criminality in the biological fathers of the controls (11 percent)
was roughly similar to that observed in the adoptive fathers.

The next step was to examine the independent contribution of criminality in the biological and adoptive fathers to
criminality in the sons. If neither the biological nor
adoptive father was criminal, or if just the adoptive father
but not the biological father was criminal, then only 11
to 12 percent of the adoptees would be called criminal--

virtually the same as the 9 percent rate observed in the
nonadopted controls. However, if the biological father was
criminal but the adoptive father was not, twice as many
adoptees had criminal records--22 percent. And if both
fathers were criminal, then 36 percent of the adoptees had
criminal records. This suggests, but hardly proves, that the
environment of a criminal father may increase criminality
only when the heredity is positive for criminality.

Hutchings and Mednick went further. They matched 143
criminal adoptees with 143 noncriminal adoptees in terms of
age and social class. Since both groups were moved to their
adoptive homes at an average age of 6 months and since in
both groups the adoption became final at the same age (one
and a half years), it is not easily argued that delayed or
irresponsible adoption was the critical factor linking the
criminality of the biological fathers to similar behavior
in their adopted offspring. The authors examined the biological parents of these two groups. Forty-nine percent of the
criminals had biological fathers who were criminal, and only
23 percent had adoptive fathers who were criminal. Of
adoptees in the control group, 10 percent had a criminal
father as an adoptive father, and 28 percent had a criminal
father as a biological father. The observed criminality of
biological mothers did not affect the results. Using multiple regression techniques, they observed that independent
contributions were made by the following three factors:
first, criminality in a biological parent; second, criminality in an adoptive parent; and third, psychiatric diagnosis
in a biological mother.

In support of Mednick's and Hutchings' work, all of nine
available twin studies indicate that homozygous twins are
two to three times as likely to be concordant for criminality as dyzygous twins (Christiansen, 1968). Also in support
of Mednick's finding that biological factors may play a role
in delinquency, the Gluecks found that 60 percent of their
delinquent youths, and only 30 percent of their nondelinquent
sample, were mesomorphs (Glueck 1950). The significance of
this finding remains to be established.

Just as Mednick's data provide the best evidence thus
far for the hereditary etiology of sociopathy, the Gluecks'
data provide the best evidence that defective mothering
plays an important role. In their own explanation of their

work, the Gluecks were impressed by many other possible etiological factors. For example, 40 percent (or eight times
the number) of delinquents had been put in foster homes as
had the controls; indifferent fathers (60 percent) and multiple moves (54 percent) were found in three times as many
delinquents' families; and a lack of family cohesiveness
occurred in twice as many (84 percent) of the families.
Hutchings' and Mednick's data, however, cast doubt on these
factors being primary; for in their adoptees, the major effect of a delinquent father on sociopathy appears to be
mediated genetically. Nevertheless, if one lives with such
a father, the likelihood of his disrupting the household is
considerable; and this (as Robins has documented) explains the
environmental differences noted among children who live with
delinquent fathers as compared with those who do not.

The ideal documentation of the effects of nurture would
have been provided by studying prospectively the adoptive
families in Mednick's sample. Certain approximations, however, can be obtained from the Gluecks' prospective design.
Those approximations strongly support the fact that maternal
neglect plays a significant role in sustained delinquency.
Twenty-eight percent of the delinquents' mothers were indifferent toward their sons--a seven-fold difference from the
controls; only a three-fold difference occurred in observed
paternal disinterest. Sixty-four percent, or five times as
many mothers of delinquents as mothers of controls, were seen
as providing unsuitable supervision, and three times as many
(96 percent) delinquents' mothers were seen as providing unsuitable discipline. Using these variables, only a two-fold
difference in the fathers occurred. One quarter of the delinquents had mothers who appeared to abuse alcohol and half
had mothers who engaged in delinquent behavior--a three-fold
difference as compared to a difference only half as great
among the fathers. Half of the delinquents came from families
of more than six children, compared to 27 percent of the
controls. Although assortative mating could explain why
some sociopathic fathers would have irresponsible wives, the
fact that differences in the quality of mothering consistently exceeded problems in fathering lends support to the
Gluecks' conclusion that early environment is critical in
the development of impulsive adults.

The Gluecks' data provide a second argument for the
importance of nurture. When the father is excluded from

consideration, an equal number of alcoholics and criminals
was found among the paternal siblings and grandparents of
both delinquents and nondelinquents. This would not be
expected if hereditary factors were all-important in the
development of sociopathy. However, one and one half times
as much criminality and emotional illness and alcoholism was
found in the mother's parents and siblings. Thus, the environment in which the mothers of delinquents were raised
was more disturbed than that of the mothers of controls.
Of course, hereditary factors in the mothers must also play
a role.

In the Gluecks' data, parental loss per se did not differentiate delinquents from nondelinquents. Death and serious illness in either mother or father were equally common
in both groups. What linked "broken homes" to delinquency
was the fact that five times as much abandonment and three
times as much separation occurred due to parental deviance
in the families of the delinquents as in the controls.

The third piece of evidence selectively linking early
maternal care to adult impulsive behavior can be found in
several prospective independent prediction studies which have
validated the Gluecks' thesis that sustained delinquency can
be predicted before age 8 (Glueck and Glueck, 1974). In a
ten-year prospective study, the New York City Youth Board
rated 301 first-grade boys in a high-crime neighborhood for
three of Gluecks' predictive factors: suitable supervision
of boy by mother, consistency of discipline of boy by mother,
and family cohesiveness (Craig and Glick, 1965). On the
basis of these scales they predicted that 243 of these 301
boys would not become delinquent by 17; in fact only 3
percent did. They predicted that 33 first-graders would
become delinquent by age 17, and 85 percent did. Craig and
Glick could not make an accurate prediction for 25 boys
because their scores fell in an intermediate range. These
boys were evenly distributed between delinquent and nondelinquent groups regarding outcome. This and similar prospective predictive studies would appear to cast grave doubt
on the theses that social class or societal labeling or bad
associates are primary causes of delinquency. Effective
prediction can be made long before these last three factors
become operative.

Lee Robins' study focused on the adult subject, and
depended on less precise evidence than the Hutchings and Med-

nick and the Gluecks' studies to reconstruct the childhood.
She certainly confirmed the Gluecks' impression that the
child's grammar school behavior and environment, rather than
adolescent experiences, imprisonment, or gang membership,
predict chronic adult delinquency. For example, in her study,
28 percent of the children referred to the guidance clinic
for antisocial behavior were diagnosed as sociopathic personalities thirty years later. This was true of only 4
percent of the other children referred to the clinic. No
non-antisocial symptoms in childhood were found that predicted delinquency in adult life. For example, tics, nail-
biting, enuresis, and unexplained pain were not useful.
Antisocial symptoms in childhood, however--especially theft,
aggressiveness, running away, truancy, and impulsiveness--
correlated highly with impulsive behavior in middle life.

The second important predictor of sociopathy that Robins
isolated was a father with a positive history of arrests,
excessive drinking, chronic unemployment, desertion, and non-
support. In keeping with Mednick's emphasis on nature,
this effect appeared partly independent of whether the father
lived with the child, and paternal delinquency covaried with
many of the environmental variables cited by the Gluecks.
For example, if the father showed one or more of the above
traits, only 20 percent of the children would be well supervised, whereas if he showed none of them, 62 percent of the
children would be well supervised. Or again, if a child had
a nonsociopathic father, and yet was placed in a foster home
or became a state ward due to parental illness or accident,
then such a child was not shown to be at increased risk for
sociopathy. The one variable that Robins found to predict
sociopathy, independent of paternal delinquency and antisocial symptoms in the child, was the presence of poor supervision and/or discipline. This is entirely congruent with
the Gluecks' findings.

Robins' work is as important for the variables that it
found not to be important as for the ones it showed to be
important. First, there are enough middle-class children in
the Robins' sample so that it was possible to factor out
social class as a critical etiological factor. Second, both
Robins (1966) and the Gluecks (1950) agreed that birth injuries, head injuries, encephalitis, and physical handicaps
were not correlated with the development of delinquency if
adequate controls were included in the study. The Gluecks

(1950) noted that developmental landmarks like walking and talking did not distinguish their two groups.

Third, if parental alcoholism and antisocial behavior are held constant, a family home "broken" by illness, divorce, or death did not predict sustained impulsiveness (Robins, 1970). This is not to deny that over the short term such events will severely disrupt a child's adjustment. The important principle would appear to be that lasting defects in a child's impulse control occur either through heredity or through sustained contact with an impulsive parent. Fourth, by using appropriate controls, the Gluecks (1950) were able to show that immigrant parents and culture conflict was not associated with an increased risk of delinquency.

Studies by both the Gluecks (1943, 1950) and Lee Robins (1966, 1970) support the concept that, over time, the impulsive personality slowly improves. This concept has much to teach us about patient management. For example, if a child is chronically antisocial in grammar school, whether he is punished by reform school as in the Gluecks' study, or is supported by counseling, as in the Cambridge-Somerville (Massachusetts) study (McCord and McCord, 1959), the next fifteen years of his life, from age 10 to 25, appear rather bleak. For example, 60 percent of delinquents in the Gluecks' study went to jail at least three times between the ages of 17 and 25, and half spent half of their young adult life in jail for repeated offenses. (Many upper-class so-called "borderline" adolescents spend an equal proportion of time in mental hospitals.) Such data suggest that criminal justice and mental health could be more reasonably and efficiently administered if recidivist juveniles served long sentences in therapeutic communities, with optimum opportunity for parole, rather than in institutions. Future control of impulsive behavior could then be managed at the discretion of the court rather than by subjugating both the courts and the individual to a new trial for each fresh offense.

In a somewhat different vein, despite profoundly disturbed and deprived childhoods, the Gluecks' delinquents and Robins' sociopaths revealed at followup that they were not at very much greater risk for schizophrenia. Only 6 percent of Robins' antisocial referrals and only about 3 percent of the Gluecks' delinquents (versus 2 percent of the controls) were ever diagnosed as schizophrenic when adult. And much

of this incidence of schizophrenia can probably be explained
by misdiagnosis of sociopathic behavior, by the increased
loading in both samples for schizophrenic heredity, and by
the fact that some schizophrenics, although not particularly
delinquent in adolescence, manifest antisocial behavior in
grammar school. These findings cast doubt on the thesis
that early maternal neglect is a major etiological factor
in schizophrenia.

Finally, there seems to be a definite tendency of individuals to outgrow chronic impulsiveness. In the Gluecks'
samples of delinquents (1943, 1968), in Robins' review of
sociopaths (1970), and in this writer's review of the natural
history of drug addiction (1970), roughly 2 percent of each
sample permanently gave up gross antisocial behavior every
year. (There was no particular age at which reform was
especially likely to occur, but, statistically, the later the
onset of delinquency, the earlier the recovery.) The Gluecks'
data (1943, 1950) suggest that both the likelihood of going
to jail and certain crimes like larceny decrease each year.
For example, before age 17, 76 percent of delinquents had an
arrest rate of one per year. Only one third had such a frequent arrest rate by age 25, and only one fifth had such an
arrest rate by age 31. Larceny of all kinds showed a similar straight line decline from mid-adolescence on; after age
35, felonies were quite unusual. A major exception to the
above generalization was that alcohol-related crimes increased
steadily from age 17 until age 40; these included drunkenness, problems regarding domestic relations, and possibly
murder. In keeping with both Hutchings' and Mednick's and
Robins' data, at least one quarter of the juvenile-court-aged
children in the Gluecks' sample of delinquents were seriously
delinquent themselves.

Thus far these three studies have been discussed for
their heuristic contribution to our understanding of the
etiology of the impulsive personality. There are also five
related lessons that can be drawn from these studies. First,
etiological studies of impulsive personalities need further
clarification, but studies that lack well-matched controls
and multivariate analysis and prospective prediction, and
longitudinal perspective are unlikely to cast much light.
Many of the obvious environmental factors associated with
delinquency turn out to be etiologically adventitious.

Second, grossly disrupted childhoods predispose individuals more to antisocial and impulsive behavior than to psychotic regression. This conclusion is at variance with the retrospective studies because schizophrenics often exaggerate while sociopaths often minimize past maternal inadequacies.

Third, although alcoholism often masquerades as impulsive behavior, the etiology and treatment needs of each is different. The basis of the difference is that a majority of alcoholics, in contrast to sociopaths, do not have deprived childhoods. From both the Gluecks' and Robins' data, it is clear that sociopaths often abuse alcohol, but there is evidence (Robins, 1966; Vaillant, 1970) that in the sociopath, alcoholism is often intermittent and less often leads to chronic dependence and medical complications than in the alcoholic without a disrupted childhood. Conversely, secondary to alcoholism, previously well-adjusted adults will often manifest impulse disorders similar to those of sociopaths but their childhoods will resemble those of controls. And unlike the sociopath and the polydrug abuser, once such alcoholics stop drinking, their impulsive behavior disappears.

Fourth, in some ways recidivist criminal behavior can be looked at as delayed maturation, rather than as a permanent defect in the ego. There is little that can be done to alter quickly the natural history of antisocial behavior. Yet since it often eventually improves with or without treatment or punishment, this suggests that antisocial behavior should be regarded more as we regard adolescence and less as we regard symptomatic neurosis or truly premeditated crime. Existing data suggest that neither easier or harsher sentencing nor more intensive psychiatric treatment will be of much value. We will do well to manage the adolescent sociopath with intelligent, nonpunitive social controls that provide a mixture of supervision and creative alternatives. The Gluecks' data have shown beyond doubt that so-called reformatories may protect society, but do nothing for the inmate.

Finally, sociopaths and impulsive personalities need to find groups to which they can belong with pride. The sociopath needs to absorb more of other people than one person, no matter how loving, can ever provide. Thus, the therapeutic community at the maximum security ward of the Utah State Hospital, for example, where the inmates hold keys to both the outside and the seclusion rooms, offers more than programs that try to transform sociopaths into patients (Kiger, 1967). Sociopaths know only too well that they have harmed others, but they can meaningfully identify only with people who feel as guilty as they do. They can abandon their defenses against grief only in the presence of people equally bereaved. Only acceptance by peers can circumvent the sociopath's profound fear that he may be pitied. Only acceptance by "recovered" peers can restore his defective self-esteem.

References

Christiansen, K.O. 1968. Threshold of tolerance in various population groups illustrated by results from the Danish criminological twin study. In A.V.S. de Reuck and R. Porter (Eds.), The Mentally Abnormal Offender. Boston: Little Brown.

Craig, M.M. and Glick, S.J. 1965. A Manual of Procedures for Application of the Glueck Prediction Table. New York: Youth Board Research Institute.

Glueck, S. and Glueck E. 1943. Criminal Careers in Retrospect. New York: The Commonwealth Fund.

Glueck, S. and Glueck E. 1968. Delinquents and Nondelinquents in Perspective. Cambridge, Mass.: Harvard University Press.

Glueck S. and Glueck E. 1974. Of Delinquency and Crime. Springfield, Ill.: C. Thomas.

Glueck S. and Glueck E. 1950. Unraveling Juvenile Delinquency. New York: The Commonwealth Fund.

Hutchings, B. and Mednick, S.A. 1976. Criminality in adoptees and their adoptive and biological parents: A pilot study. In S.A. Mednick and K.O. Christiansen (Eds.), Biosocial Bases of Criminal Behavior. New York: Gardner Press.

Kiger, R.S. 1967. Treatment of the psychopath in the therapeutic community. Hosp. Community Psychiatry, 18, 191-196.

McCord, W. and McCord, J. 1959. Origins of Crime. New
    York: Columbia University Press.
Robins, L.N. 1966. Deviant Children Grown Up. Baltimore:
    Williams & Wilkins Co.
Robins, L.N. 1970. The Adult Development of the Antisocial
    Child. Seminars in Psychiatry, 1970, 2, 420-434.
Vaillant, G.E. 1970. The Natural History of Narcotic Drug
    Addiction. Seminars in Psychiatry, 2, 486-498.

Part II

Clinical Approaches

PANIC STATES AND IMPULSIVE BEHAVIOR

Howard A. Wishnie, M.D.

Assistant Clinical Professor of Psychiatry,
Harvard Medical School at The Cambridge
Hospital, Cambridge, Massachusetts and Staff
Psychiatrist, Veterans Administration Hospital,
Bedford, Massachusetts

Prior to the 1970s little time had been spent in pre-
paring psychiatrists for work with addicts, alcoholics, criminals, or sociopathic persons. Such people were then considered by many to be untreatable and were consistently excluded from psychiatric treatment settings.

The psychiatric diagnosis and problem of interest during
the 1960s was "borderline personality disorder." During my
own early experience, I concurred with fellow psychiatric
residents that this problem seemed to be limited primarily to
women who could be charming, intriguing, and explosively labile. These persons were insightful, but their insights were
of little use when they seemed caught up in emotional storms.
The thoughtful graduate student, for example, could easily
become enraged and destroy her thesis, cut her wrists, and
overdose. The shy, soft-spoken librarian could suddenly
swear like a fishwife and go off for a weekend with several
men. Male patients with such impulsiveness and lability were
rarely seen in psychiatric treatment settings.

With this clinical experience as background, I went off
to serve two years in the Public Health Service at the Lexington treatment center for narcotics addicts in Kentucky.
In 1970 this was one of two such federally sponsored centers.
The advice of friends and colleagues at that time was to find
some good books and not be concerned about the efficacy of my
clinical work for two years; for my coworkers these addicts
and criminals could not be treated. However, I was surprised
to find that both the women I had seen during residency train-

ing and the men at Lexington shared similar character
traits: labile mood swings, impulsive solutions to problems,
little capacity to see the repetitive nature of their feelings and actions, little view of their own role in creating
problems, projection of responsibility onto others, and, most
importantly, severe limitations in their abilities to establish genuine, enduring personal relationships. How could this
be? Despite their histories, these people were charming,
likable, coherent. They were not deluded, yet periodically
their behavior exploded and jeopardized existing relationships. No one could remain closely tied to such people.

The dynamics of defenses that included projection, projective identification, distortion, denial, and splitting
were abundantly present in these individuals; no insufficiency
of "material" here. The problem was to find a way to communicate with angry, alienated people who had no use for or interest in dealing with me or their own situations. In their
view, they didn't need help; their problems, as they saw them,
lay in the society, their race, or family, or wife, or girlfriend. The destructive, antisocial nature of their behavior
appeared to have nothing to do with them.

How could we then begin to find a common meeting ground
that would allow mutual and useful exploration? As I and
others talked and lived with these men in Kentucky, a number
of issues became clearly observable. The men continually
repeated the same kinds of struggles and charades within the
institution that they had created for themselves in the
streets, and they seemed unaware that last week's argument or
fight was just like the one this week. In fact, these struggles also replicated those they had experienced with wives,
parents, teachers, and employers outside of the hospital.

Paradoxically, these men, who were constantly conning and
deceiving, ever alert to new ploys and sometimes obsessed
with oneupmanship, presented extremely clear, unambiguous psychological material. Although they did not believe there was
any validity to the notion of their own internal emotional
states, they made statements which were very clear to someone
with psychological awareness. To the men, however, these
clear revelations seemed inconsequential. Rather, they focused on the most literal and legalistic aspects of their
lives, and tended to deny the way they actually felt about
current and past events, and hence continued to shrink from
the meaning of their feelings and situations.

The following example demonstrates this psychological transparency.

> Gerry came to his staffing conference one half hour late, yawning, and casually said, "Gee, Doc, if you wanted me here on time, you should have had a nurse wake me up." He sat down with his shirt hanging out and fly open. Smiling and joking with the staff, he asked us to go on. As his history of childhood desperation was reviewed, he seemed to shift about uncomfortably and said that this stuff was unimportant. "In fact, Doc, I had a great time as a kid. I was free, man. Other guys had to be home and I could stay out as long as I wanted. No one cared." As the facts continued to emerge we heard that Gerry had once been trapped in a storm drain for several days and was only rescued when the police heard his cries. In fact, no one did care. He seemed more distraught when the seriousness of this issue was mentioned and again tried to cover it with a joke that this was the greatest adventure of his life. He attempted to react in similar fashion to the fact that he was given to a stranger at the age of 9. The more that was mentioned, however, the more he shifted about, the more he looked away, the more he tried to deny the effect of such experience. When he became disruptive in the meeting I quietly said that it was no wonder he wanted a nurse to wake him and help him dress. It was clear that his mother had been too preoccupied to pay much attention to him, and he seemed to need to know that someone cared. Perhaps that was why his actions asked that we give him the care he denied wanting. Gerry, the tough, wise-cracking, penitentiary-hardened man was actually crying; his actions implored us to tell him, "Button your shirt, zip your fly." Continued questions and comments gradually elicited more of what he felt went on within him.

This brief case excerpt illustrates that alienated, hard-to-reach people can be helped to scrutinize their internal life states even when they are most resistant.

If in fact these men had problems observing their own behavior and seeing it in a useful way, so did professionals. During the 1970s hospitals and clinics began to attempt treatment of those previously diagnosed as untreatable. In response to new social and legislative mandates, professionals

began trying to develop separate and expert treatment facilities. Community psychiatric services, alcoholism services,
narcotics treatment centers, polydrug treatment centers, and
in some places centers for the treatment of severely impulsive people increased or were developing for the first time.
However, like the blind man touching the elephant and describing the entirety in terms of his limited observation, we
provided treatment in a fragmented way. Each group of professionals focusing on a particular problem became "expert"
in the treatment of the particular symptom manifestation.
With but some exceptions, few people could see the whole
elephant. The multifaceted nature of the problem is illustrated by the following example.

     Jim, age 19, first came to my attention just as I
began working at a comprehensive mental health treatment center. He had just been admitted to the inpatient psychiatric service after an overdose of drugs.
He allegedly became depressed when his girlfriend left
him, and this was given as the reason for the overdose
necessitating hospitalization. After a few days on the
ward he seemed to be his usual self--angry, demanding,
nasty, and provocative. He showed little inclination to
question the reasons for his own behavior; he just wanted
out. The problem was us; he would be O.K. if he could
be discharged. The facts--that he had just been discharged from the Army with an undesirable discharge, had
no goals, no job, no direction and no place to live, that
he had overdosed, and that he had lost the one relationship he claimed to value--all of this was old history for
him, and he had no interest in discussing it. He was
discharged on the third day against medical advice with
a diagnosis of transient depressive reaction in an
adolescent suffering a character disorder.

     He next appeared in our system when he was arrested
for assault and sent to jail for several months. He
received a new diagnosis--this time from the criminal
justice system. He was a delinquent, "nasty son-of-a-
bitch." They had seen a lot like him and would probably
see him again. Several months later, I again met Jim in
the alcoholism treatment unit of the same mental health
system where he had been admitted. The staff there told
us that the psychiatry service had overlooked his major
problem--alcoholism. Everything else was secondary to

this. I encountered Jim once again the next year while
consulting to a drug treatment unit where he was being
treated for multiple drug abuse. Yet again I was told
that those who had worked with Jim previously had not
had an accurate perspective: he was most importantly a
polydrug abuser and that should have been his treatment
focus. Over the next year, Jim appeared in various parts
of the community mental health and legal system--jails,
hospitals, and clinics. While we continued to dispute
the diagnosis and treatment approach, Jim settled the
issue. He came to the hospital D.O.A. as a result of an
overdose.

The importance of this clinical vignette and its horror
lies in the fact that each of us did in fact see a facet of
Jim's behavior and problem. What we failed to see and deal
with adequately was that no matter what his mode of presentation, whether to the police or to one of the various clinics, Jim's way of behaving never really changed. He would
choose a different <u>means</u> of manifesting his problem but the
underlying dynamics of his behavior remained the same. The
mental health approach that focuses only on a particular symptom manifestation and mistakes it for the entire problem is
similar to treating a fever with aspirin while the underlying pneumonia continues unabated.

Panic States and Impulsive Behavior

The crucial issue becomes that of developing a useful
concept that allows us to focus on the underlying character
problem, regardless of the current or most prominent symptom. As I continued to make observations at Lexington and
later in Boston, in hospital and in clinic settings, one
theme seemed consistently to underlie impulsive behavior:
the existence of a panic state. Whether the person used
drugs or alcohol, cut his wrists, or assaulted others seemed
of little consequence in treatment; various behavioral manifestations were secondary. Each time I look at the precipi-
tant factor of a piece of behavior, I was struck with the fact
that a panic-filled moment preceded the outburst.

For purposes of this discussion, impulsive behavior can
be defined as those actions which are rapidly conceived and
carried out with poor planning and little thought as to the

consequences. Frequently the behavior places the individual
in a more difficult situation than the one from which he began. In retrospect, the individual may reflect that he "was
not thinking," or "a strong feeling (of panic) came over him."

> Jack was leaning against the ping-pong table when
> Henry asked him to move. Instantly and automatically
> Jack refused and challenged Henry to move him. Jack,
> who had only a short time to go before discharge from
> the institution, risked being killed by Henry or being
> sent back to prison. He later explained that he knew
> Henry was really implying that he, Jack, was short
> (5'4") and he, Henry (6'2"), could lord it over him and
> boss him around. "Man, I know I'm nothing!" he said with
> great intensity and agitation," but if these suckers
> find out, I'm finished. I had to fight him, I had to
> stand my ground. No one's going to do that to me." To
> those who observed the incident, Henry was in fact not
> lording it over Jack. It was Jack's sensitivity about
> his size and its meaning--that he was nothing, small,
> vulnerable, and weak--that caused him to react. He
> panicked in that instant.

The panic state may be described in two ways:

1. The individual who is characteristically prone to
panic usually functions by seeing all of his life's difficulties emanating from other people, institutions, and systems. Thus he might say: "If my wife hadn't done this to me
or reacted in that way, I would be O.K." Or, "He shouldn't
have come at me when I had a gun; it's his fault I shot him."
"He should have known better." Or "If they made drugs legal,
I'd be O.K." Such an individual accepts no personal role in
the events of his life; he is the victim reacting in self-
defense. Periodically such a person is suddenly confronted
with the fact that he sees himself as worthless, powerless,
and weak--a total nothing, vulnerable to everyone. This
sense of utter worthlessness and vulnerability generates an
unbearable anxiety that leads to massive panic which the person must rid himself of quickly. He does this by explosively
blaming and assaulting others.

2. Conceptualized simply within a psychodynamic framework, the panic state occurs when a system of defenses based
upon projective identification suddenly collapses. The individual is overwhelmed by the previous projected, but now

internalized, negative self-image. This internalized, negative self-image leads the individual to feel totally devalued,
demeaned, and worthless. He reacts automatically--without
thought--and attempts to reproject this negative view of
himself. The automatic attempt at reprojection comprises the
impulsive behavior.

The conceptualization of these mechanisms can be illustrated by the following diagrams, which were developed in
group sessions with men who had spent a great deal of time in
prisons and penitentiaries. These individuals had difficulty
using verbal interchanges and seemed to need a conceptualiza-
zation that was visual, clear, and simple. The basic diagram
is shown in Figure 1. The large rectangle represents the
total individual; the area to the left of the rectangle his
current reality; the area to the right the developmental input of his early life. Within the rectangle itself there are

The Individual

	External View of Self	Defenses against awareness of internal view	Internal View of Self	
Current Reality	How others see me		"The real me"	Developmental Input
	Traits			
	Habits			
	Attitudes		Negative beliefs	
	Character behavior		Doubts about self	
	Appearance		Questions about self	
2	1a	1b	1c	3

Part 1a, the left side of the rectangle reflects the appearance the individual hopes
to convey to the world about him.
Part 1b, reflects the defenses against full awareness by the individual of his personal doubts and beliefs about himself.
Part 1c, pictures the individual's internal view of himself. This view is generally
avoided by the individual and hidden from those about him.
Part 2, the space to the left of Figure, represents events and influences in the individual's current reality that impinge upon him.
Part 3, the space to the right of Figure, represents the area of developmental
influences that impinged on him in the past.

Figure 1

three subdivisions. The left-hand area represents the external view of the self, "how the others see me," as the men
would say. It includes one's traits, habits, attitudes, character, behavior, and appearance. The small central area,
shown with dotted lines, represents those defenses that keep
the individual from being aware of his doubts and negative beliefs about himself. The area to the right, or the internal
view of the self, is one which impulsive individuals frequently deny exists and spend a great deal of time avoiding.
It might be called "the real me" by the individual, and con-
tains his beliefs and doubts about himself, his questions and
conflicts.

Figure 2 presents the basic picture of how the individual
interprets his behavior: a situation occurs in the current
reality, it impinges on the external character (how the individual views himself), and he responds. To him it is a
simple, cut-and-dried matter.

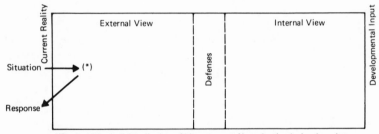

*The inpulsive individual's view of his responses. Note that he denies the existence
of his defense, internal motivations, and past. He also sees his response as propor-
tionate.

Figure 2

Figures 3 and 4 present a more accurate picture of what
underlies impulsive behavior. An event occurs in the environment. Its meaning cuts through the external image,
through defenses, and touches negative beliefs within the individual until a panic state develops. Once the panic occurs
(and this can be instantaneous) the individual reacts explosively. (Thus the darkened arrow: behavior can move in two
directions. It can be directed externally into the environment, in a massive destructive rage directed against others;
or it can be directed against the externalized self, as in

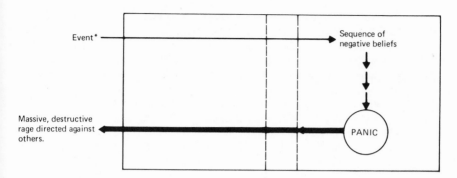

Figure 3

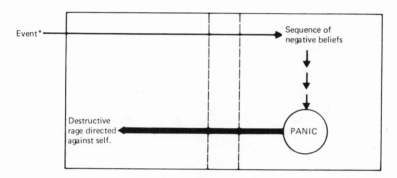

Figure 4

overdosing, wrist cutting, frantic sexual behavior, or any
form of behavior which relieves the anxiety and externalizes
from the internal self. Figure 4 is almost the same as
Figure 3, except in the locus of the externalization.   A
situation occurs and touches internal doubts. It then leads
to the development of anxiety, depression, and finally panic.
There is then an exaggerated response with impulsivity directed against the external self.

     The reality and usefulness of this visual approach may
be best illustrated by actual clinical material.

     Vic was a 28-year-old, black high school dropout,
     born and raised in a poor section of a moderate-sized
     northern city. His family was large and under constant

financial stress. He entered a treatment center after
being acquitted of homicide. (He had, in fact, committed
the murder.) His mood fluctuated from superficial
friendliness to cool hostility. He presented himself as
an angry, black nationalist who was sensitive to any real
or inferred racial slight, and justified all his outbursts as resulting from external circumstances. Several incidents, however, helped uncover more of his internal perspective.

During one group therapy session the group focused on
a serious argument that had resulted in a fight. Vic
and Paul (another angry black man) were dividing up the
cleaning of the ward lounge. It was Vic's turn to sweep
the floor while Paul polished it. Vic did not want to
sweep the floor. He stated defiantly that he just didn't
want to and no one could make him do it. His two-part
statement shifted the focus from the personal conflict
to a struggle in terms of "you can't make me." In fact,
a struggle ensued over the issue of who was stronger.
Both men reached for baseball bats and had to be re-
strained by staff and group members. In therapy, Vic
was asked why he disliked the job so much. He became annoyed and again tried a diversion about institutions and
being "fucked over." For a long time he was silent,
staring angrily at the therapist and Paul. We continued
to question him about what all of this meant. After
all, other men on the unit did the job; it was rotated.
What was his reason? Finally, in exasperation, he said,
"I just wouldn't clean up that shit. Man, that's a shitty job." Further questioning and constant references
to the job as shitty led to the understanding that the
piles of dust, dirt, and wax actually reminded him of
shit. There was a tense silence as he stated this. His
face and jaw tightened as he articulated this explanation. He seemed to be flooded with thoughts and feelings. We continued talking. "So it's shit, so what.
What's that matter? Everybody cleans it up." He paused
as if lost in thought, and as he spoke I commented that
his appearance and tone had changed. We began diagram-
ming. During the discussion that followed, words and
phrases were added to the diagram (Figure 5) by mutual
consent of the group and Vic. He was given the option
of changing any statement in the diagram, substituting
his own comments when there was a disagreement.

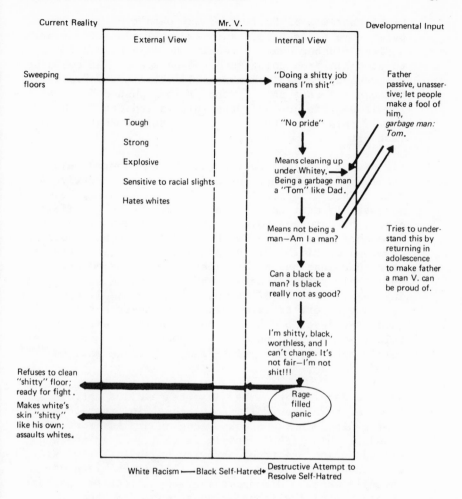

Figure 5

He went on to say quietly that he was having memories.
When he was a child his home was visited at Christmas
by whites who brought charity packages. He remembered
their patronizing comments about how nicely the apartment was fixed up. "It was really a shitty place, but
they were so nice [said sarcastically] to us poor blacks."
He was furious with his father for not having "enough
pride" to throw them out; he hated them.

His father was an Uncle Tom; why wasn't he a man?
Later some pipes burst, and sewage flooded the basement.
A black plumber came to repair the damage, and Vic tried
to stop him from going into the basement. He could not
understand how a black man could voluntarily "wade
through all that shit." The plumber pushed by, explain-
ing it was his job and "the shit washed off." Did Vic
really think that there were some things that did not
wash off?

Vic paused and then continued. He remembered being
ashamed of his father for not being more assertive at
home. He could recall times when, as a child, he was
excessively critical of his father. Later, in adolescence, he returned home to try to help his father become more assertive--"Be the man of the house, so I could
be proud of him." His hope had been to create the family
structure that had never existed. When asked why, he
could only respond that for him, something was missing
inside. It was as if he couldn't go on in life without
one last effort to gain what he had never had in childhood. He described his father, and in a tearful rage,
told that he was a passive man, who though strong, let
people make a fool of him--"man, a garbage man, an Uncle
Tom."

He then recalled that he had often avoided certain sections of town when walking to school in order to avoid
seeing his father and acknowledging him in front of his
friends. His father was, in fact, a garbage man who
walked behind the truck throwing trash in. Vic said, "He
was cleaning up under Whitey. I'll never clean up
Whitey's shit." His excessive sensitivity to real or
imagined racial slights or questions of manhood made
sense in terms of being both black and a man. His fears
of being like the father, whom he loved, began to emerge.

Exploration of an ordinary dispute through associative
techniques began giving us insight into Vic's motivation and
self-image. He touched upon his own doubts about being a man.
All of these issues were succinctly stated with the help of
the diagram. Yet the role of panic wasn't quite clear.
Weeks later, at a staffing conference, the basic, previously
hidden beliefs came to light.

Vic had been discussing a time in his life when he had
supported himself by brutal assaults. He casually noted
as an afterthought that all of his victims had been
white--not only white, but fair-skinned, blond, blue-
eyed, tall, and thin. During that period Vic was in a
situation where he had access to servicemen leaving an
active-duty base. He would meet these men at an airport
where they awaited rides home. As we tried to get him
to describe his actual behavior he became annoyed and
tried to avoid this. With our insistence, he began telling how he would pose as a friendly, not too bright,
black [a lame position], and he would meet the whites in
bars. He would then arrange for drugs, women, gambling,
homosexual activity, or whatever they wanted. The gul-
lible white would then accompany Vic to his apartment.
When they were safely inside, a confederate would knock
on the door, saying that there were police outside and
that they had to leave. Vic would hustle the victim out
of a back door into an alley and although armed with a
pistol, Vic would pick up a bat that he had waiting and
beat the man with it. Again he began shifting in his
chair and seemed uncomfortable. When asked for details, Vic uncomfortably stated that it wasn't important; why should he talk about it. "What did you do?"
"Man, I hit him." "Where?" "I hit him in the face.
It's not important." "Tell me anyway." "Shit, man, I
hit him in the nose, that's all." "Just the nose?" He
glanced away uncomfortably and fidgeted. "Why do we have
to discuss this?" "It seems important." "No, man, I
beat 'em up good--the nose, the mouth, the jaw."

I commented that it seemed foolish to take the extra
time to beat up the man and risk detection, when he
could have used the knife or gun on him much more quickly and quietly. Angrily Vic said there was no particular reason, but he agreed it was stupid. I then quietly
began mulling over the circumstances--tall, thin, blond,
blue-eyed whites. "For no reason, a man as clever as
you, who usually is quite careful, takes the risk of a
person screaming out, yelling, and getting you caught.
It sounds stupid to me. A bat across the nose, hitting
him in the face--it just doesn't make any sense, Vic."
As I made these comments, Vic glared at me silently,
looking increasingly furious. "What are you thinking?"
"I'm just picturing you there on the ground with your

face beat in." "What do I look like?" Already sen-
sing the answer, I pushed. "Your nose is flat, your
cheeks and lips are puffed out and bloody, your . . .,"
and he stopped. His facial expression changed in apparent amazement. "Who has a flat nose, puffy cheeks and
lips?" Vic paused and did not answer. "Did you think
of that while you were assaulting your victims?" Quietly, in a trancelike voice and with little awareness of
others in the room, he said, "Their skin, their smooth
white skin. I made them as shitty and ugly as me."

Little more needed to be said at that time. In subsequent weeks we were able to define the kind of panic that
Vic experienced. When he murdered the man whose homicide he
had been acquitted of, the circumstances were similar. He
felt the man had made a fool of him. He began feeling worthless and like nothing. He had to kill the man. "I had to
kill that motherfucker--if I didn't I was nothing. It had
to be; I couldn't stand it."

We continued to talk and found that Vic believed that
being black meant he was always ugly and shitty. In later
discussions he talked about the fury he felt at being burdened with this unfair disadvantage he couldn't overcome. If
they didn't respect him, at least they would fear him. Could
a black be a man? Could he be a man?

Clearly Vic was responding in large part to the reality
of black status in society. However, his specific behavior
was motivated by an internal perception of himself as being
second-rate, shitty, black. He expected all whites to automatically view him as inferior and resented what he really
was. As he saw it, he would never even have a chance to prove
himself. The man he had murdered had, of course, been white.
He felt he had to erase this person's existence because it was
evidence of his own inferiority. That man represented all
those laughing, white motherfuckers--a projection--"If they
can't respect me, they damn well will fear me."

In further disputes, we were always able to uncover that
the panic Vic felt was related to his feeling worthless and
black, and had caused him to explode against people. Over
time he began to view whites as individuals, not as a homo-
geneous group, and became friendly with several on the staff.
He once related imagining a particular white staff member as

his mother. His hatred diminished greatly, and in tense
situations we noted that he was no longer prone to explosive
outbursts: he was less vulnerable to seeing himself as
worthless.

The story of Vic illustrates another issue in the treatment of such individuals, namely, the response of the therapist. The preceding presentation cannot convey the kinds of
feelings I experienced in working with this man--the initial
fear, the response to his rage and hurt, the sense I had of
wanting to withdraw and avoid what was going on, the wish to
make some kind of deal to get rid of such people, to lock them
up--apprehensions common to all who work with explosive people. Over time, however, as Vic became more of a human being
to himself and to us, we were able to talk about that crucial panic. All of this work occurred in groups of individuals, both black and white, all with long prison records--
records of multiple assault and brutal behavior toward each
other. In such a setting one is usually not able to explore
such issues safely. We were able to do so because the staff
conveyed interest and respect for the men. Personal issues
were examined in detail because we shared the conviction
that the most painful memories and feelings contained meaning from which we might be able to learn.

An individual's sense of feeling totally worthless and
vulnerable can be aroused by a facial gesture, vocal intona-
tion, brief verbal expression, or the denial of a particular goal. The sense of being worthless, and thus vulnerable,
is experienced as an attack from outside the self. As a result, the individual seeks to retaliate or control what he
sees as the source of the attack. Because he is constantly
vulnerable to such feelings, he expends much of his energy
warding off this feeling state.

In the work described here, the destructive reaction is
clarified and the individual is helped to see that his sensitivity results from an internalized belief in his own worthlessness. Approaching the issue logically, without moral
judgment or entrapment in side issues, helps the individual
focus upon the sequence of events. Thus, the patient and
therapist are allied in the process of thoughtful reconstruc-
tion.

Once the individual begins to see his behavior as a repeated pattern with sequential steps, he is ready to consider

that his overreactions and excessive sensitivity are internally motivated. In this situation one can inquire as to what
it was the individual felt when he experienced the sense of
total devaluation. At such a time the person relives, in
the therapy, the increasing anxiety and crescendo to panic.
Again, the therapist focuses in a supportive yet determined
way on the person's exact description of the feelings. He
does not allow euphemisms or summary statements like, "It
just feels bad, man." Instead, he pursues in great detail the
specifics of feeling "bad." At this time the patient is
open to remembering early experiences with this feeling and
can reconstruct the origin of this sense of worthlessness
and panic.

Individuals who have stayed in treatment for several
years have been able to reconstruct these experiences, going
back as far as the first year of their lives. The sense of
abandonment and fragmentation of the self is clearly related
to early disruptions in the mother-child relationship. The
process of reconstructing these events in a setting that
respects the individual's dignity necessitates consistent and
caring persons who can aid in constructing a sense of personal worth.

WOMEN THERAPISTS AND IMPULSIVE VIOLENT PATIENTS

Lenore A. Boling, M.D.

Associate Psychiatrist, McLean Hospital, Belmont, Massachusetts, and Assistant Professor of Psychiatry at McLean Hospital, Harvard Medical School, Boston, Massachusetts

Several approaches to violence are common to most cultures. Among them are punishment, containment, and channelling of aggression. Retaliation, protection, and sometimes hope of change are elements in these interventions. In our own individualistic society there is, historically, a good deal of ambivalence concerning expectations and sanctions in regard to harming others. It is generally accepted that an individual has choices; but if he wants to get anywhere he has to search out opportunities, make his presence felt, compete and win. There are moral and legal constraints on the degree and methods of competition, but also an unspoken admiration and envy of those who circumvent these limits. Just one example of this is documented in Matthew Josephson's book, The Robber Barons, which describes the careers of a few men who amassed great fortunes and power on the fringes of dishonesty and public acceptance. We balance on a fine line between the use and misuse of aggression. However, uncontrolled aggression, and particularly physical violence, is not generally accepted and is considered "bad" except under certain ritualized circumstances. Yet we are aware to varying degrees of the potential presence of aggression in ourselves. Each, according to his biological and environmental experience, makes what peace he can with this valued and devalued attribute. For the most part, it is kept out of conscious awareness. Nonetheless, violence is a subject which has been attracting an increasing amount of attention in recent years.

Confrontation with aggression in others arouses shock, fear, and excitement. It restimulates our own aggressive instincts; it gnaws at our carefully constructed defenses against it; it is at great odds with our image of ourselves as altruistic, or at least conflict-avoiding, individuals. In the helping professions these defenses and this image reach their peak. If one conceives of violent behavior as something to be understood and even "treated" (a medical term implying illness), then the one who treats must do two things: internally modify the carefully instilled conviction that this behavior is merely "bad"; and, simultaneously, deal with the existence of these unacceptable impulses in himself or herself. Both of these difficulties naturally often result in avoidance as an immediate anxiety-reducing solution. Papers by Lion, Azcarate, and Arana (1974) and Lion and Pasternak (1973) address themselves to the propensity of professionals for avoiding violent patients.

Yet another conflict on a more conscious level is involved. What is the responsibility of the helping professional to the individual as opposed to his responsibility to society? Can they be seen as the same? Considerable empathic and intellectual effort at moments of crisis is required to recognize that they are the same, and that protecting society is also in fact protecting the patient. Thus it is often the case that the patient is the last person to be considered when he comes or is brought for evaluation or treatment.

First the physician must deal with his own reaction. Then he may be required to answer to society. He may be faced with pressures from family, community, court, school, employers, or other groups and individuals. Both of these requirements appear to be in opposition to his usual approach to a patient. He is trained to concentrate on the patient immediately and to ignore or hold in abeyance personal and societal considerations. In the case of the threatening or violent patient, however, prevention of destructive action assumes a first-rank priority. A glance at the literature reveals many attempts to identify and assess danger signals, to predict violent behavior, and to suggest methods of coping with it. Menninger and Modlin (1971), Lion and his associates (1968, 1969, 1976), and others have organized and communicated their experience along these lines. Their purpose in so doing, however, appears to be an effort to present to people who work with these patients a tool that will in some

degree free them from their own initial, regression-promoting
anxieties and thus allow them to address themselves to the
need and frequent desperation of the patients. In other
words, this may permit them to regain the higher-level defenses, including sublimation, which have brought them to
their professional commitment in the first place.

In the light of the nature of the conflicts just described, if one adds the pervasive notion held until recently
(and, I might note, still largely unrelinquished) of the
female as the passive, peacemaking source of comfort and
nourishment, the female member of a helping profession in
our society may in fact be in the most conflictful position
of all with regard to dealing with aggression. (I shall in
the future use the term "therapist" to denote the "helping
professional," partly to avoid the clumsiness of the latter
term and partly to emphasize the fact that, whatever the
professional role, the intent is therapeutic.)

The female therapist, while partaking of the more general
"images" of what a therapist may be and do, also has a special
place in the imaginations of the professional staff and the
public at large. In my experience, female therapists have
been variously imagined to be: the small, firm, gentle
woman who powerfully and magically can control the wildest
patient with a few words or by her very presence; the mother-
ly, understanding woman who can appeal to a patient's softer
longings and feelings and thus calm him down; the weak,
vulnerable woman who must be protected from dangerous patients; the immune woman who will be treated with respect
by male patients no matter how angry or out of control the
patient may feel; the person in authority who will nonetheless have to call upon male brawn for help; the incompetent
person who will be completely unable to deal with a potentially explosive situation. These are fairly common responses,
and there are numerous examples of institutional myths and
stories of the first two types. Not infrequently, male mental
health workers or custodial personnel can be seen shepherd-
ing women staff members through wards or clinics, warning
them, standing guard, and so forth. Many nursing staffs
function with the implicit understanding that, while the head
nurse (female) is in charge of the ward and may even provide
instructions in techniques of dealing with violent patients,
mental health workers (male) will be called upon when actual
physical violence is anticipated or in progress.

On the inpatient services of mental hospitals, the ratio
of male to female staff on each shift is an important consideration in estimating the capacity of a ward to deal with
certain behaviors. In interesting contrast to this observation are the data presented by Levy and Harticollis (1976)
comparing the number of instances of violent behavior in a
therapeutic milieu staffed entirely by females with that on
a conventionally staffed ward. The ratio was 0 to 13, respectively, during one year's time. The authors hypothesize that
controlled confrontation can resolve conflict and is dangerous only if there is "intent and reciprocal expectation of
violence." They point out that in primate and primitive
human societies, order is maintained through the power of the
males and that the male aid's role as masculine authority is
"based on the intent to do violence."

All of the above images are based on socially accepted
stereotypes of the female, both as a powerful and a powerless figure. What is the female therapist's image of herself
in relation to aggressive patients? How does she reconcile
the necessities of her job with these stereotypes? For instance, some patients are known or thought to respond to firm
and controlling limits. This is a role which, even in our
changing society, is not one that is highly valued for women.

Together with the "normal stress" of making professional
decisions appropriate to the situation, a female therapist
has additional internal and external burdens. Some individuals may be temperamentally, or by indoctrination, incapable
of asserting themselves in this way. Those who do find themselves able and willing to accept this responsibility may
have to settle within themselves the problem of what sets
them apart from other women and how to integrate this aspect
or aspects of their personalities. They may ask themselves
how and why they resemble or differ from important female
figures in their lives. On the one hand, there are expectations that the woman do the job, whatever it may require;
on the other hand, there are expectations that she cannot and
should not do the job. Included in this area, of course,
are the well-known problems of adjusting to a situation in
which the female therapist is demonstrating equal competence
with men and even competing with them in the professional
arena.

Within herself, the woman must struggle with the question of what it means to help a patient with issues of con-

trol. If this requires that at times she apply this control
to herself, what pictures spring unbidden to mind?--a cruel
and powerful female commander of a prison camp? an asexual
soldier fighting shoulder to shoulder with men? We are clearly speaking of the potential arousal of dark, aggressive, and
perhaps sadistic impulses which may be even more threatening
to women than to men. These questions, however, all pre-
suppose a successful intervention. What if psychological
methods fail? Can she physically protect herself or others?

It should be noted that a male must deal with the con-
verse of this problem: it is expected that he will meet
aggression with aggression. Can his masculinity withstand
the insult of attack without the possibility of response in
kind? Might he be provoked to retaliation and hurt the patient physically? Might he find himself in a confrontation
for which he is physically ill-prepared and temperamentally
unsuited?

A therapist has chosen a style and work setting that
should enable measured, considered responses rather than action and spontaneity. Both male and female are subject to
the narcissistic injury that attack entails, not to mention
the possibility of physical injury as well. I would like
to add that all of these fantasies and conflicts are not
merely hypothetical. I have experienced some of them myself
and I have heard all of them expressed by a large number of
individuals whose work I have supervised.

It should be mentioned, of course, that there are specific responses that may be elicited in the individual therapist, depending on his or her own experience in life. This
necessitates making careful distinctions between the reality
of the treatment situation and the fears, fantasies, and
wishes in the therapist. With increasing exposure it is to
be hoped that one will become familiar with those elements
in particular situations that come from oneself. The therapist can learn to identify those events and behaviors that
arouse his or her own strongest feelings, particularly those
that resonate with the patient's apparent feeling state.
Awareness of all these factors in advance of the time they
arise in an actual situation provides the therapist with an
important advantage. (Anticipation and preparedness are,
in fact, techniques that many of us try to impart to impulsive patients to help them cope with their poorly understood

urges.) It facilitates the ability to separate reality from
fantasy.

In addition, it is helpful to recognize one's own mechanisms for coping with stress. I can remember examples in
my own career when I have utilized denial, projection, isolation of affect, and rationalization—among other defenses—
to protect myself in threatening situations. In retrospect,
it is possible to reflect on how useful they have been and,
conversely, what opportunities may have been obliterated by
their use. Indeed I can think of instances early on in my
career when the prevention of violence was more a function
of the patient's defenses than of my own. Some questions it
may be necessary to confront include: Do you tend to withdraw
from the situation, take flight, find a way to escape without
loss of face? Do you ignore danger signals? Do you find
yourself taking deliberate risks that even go across your
grain? (One person's courage is another person's counter-
phobia, depending on whether one applies psychopathologic
interpretations across the board.) As a woman do you readily
accede to expectations of dependence? Or do you, on the contrary, stubbornly resist any reaction that suggests dependency, ignoring real and present dangers, and thus limit your
opportunities for action? A so-called normal person can use
a variety of defenses in stressful situations. Recognition
of the ones most usual for each therapist and consideration
of their origins and consequences are steps toward mastery
and increasing options.

Thus far I have been addressing the subject of the "baggage" that the therapist brings with him (and in this case,
with her, particularly) to the encounter with the violent
patient. This involves issues of countertransference in the
broadest sense. Usually discussion of countertransference
tends to be considered at the end of case studies. In the
matter of direct threat of violence, it is of such great
importance, so ubiquitous and so urgent, that it deserves
immediate attention and constant vigilance, especially until
the therapist has achieved some degree of comfort with this
phenomenon. In my experience, the sorting-out process must
begin at the first moment one even hears about the patient.
Whether verbal or written, these communications often arouse
feelings of alarm and urgency that seem to call for some sort
of instant action on the part of the recipient. If the situation allows, it is helpful to get as much amplification as

possible of the facts, not only about the precipitating event that culminates in the patient's being placed in one's care, but also about the broader life situation of the person and of important individuals in his life. This serves a two-fold purpose. It casts some light on the state of mind and motivation of those involved in the patient's social network, including those who have referred him. It also adds a dimension to one's perception and understanding of the patient; he becomes more of a person and less of a walking threat. This facilitates the development of empathy and also allows for the beginning of a rational consideration of the degree of threat that the patient actually poses and to whom.

One can then begin to ask the questions: Is this a person with a documented reputation for violence? How recently? Does he merely possess a rumored potential for violence? Does he have a history of or fear of loss of control? Is he only angry, or afraid, or both, or possibly verbally abusive? Is someone else angry at him? Has he cause for depression? Is someone provoking him to violence? Papers by Lion, Madden and Christopher (1976), Macdonald (1967), and Menninger and Modlin (1971), among others, are of practical assistance in providing lists of factors crucial to this assessment. All agree on the importance of past history of homicide or assaults, recent frustrations or threats to self-esteem, ambivalent and particularly sadomasochistic relationships with important persons and, of course, diagnosis.

Violent behavior has been documented in patients suffering from psychosis (schizophrenia, manic-depressive illness, paranoid states); in patients with a large variety of character disorders, all of which may have a salient component of poor impulse control and low frustration tolerance; and in patients with organic brain dysfunction. Some investigators say that at least some minimal degree of organic impairment can be found in many patients diagnosed as having personality disorders. Several studies indicate a high correlation of violent behavior with a history of emotional deprivation or rejection in childhood; parental seduction; exposure to brutality in childhood (particularly in parents); and, in the patient himself, the familiar triad of childhood fire-setting, cruelty to animals and other children, and enuresis.

Attention to the patient's history leads us to a consideration of the baggage that he brings to the situation
with the therapist. The setting in which he is seen is of
considerable significance. For example, my own experience
has been chiefly on the inpatient services of mental hospitals. This in itself is a special setting with certain implications for patient and staff. The patient has already
gone through some sort of screening process. Not only has
he or someone else identified him as someone in need of
evaluation, treatment, and possibly temporary separation from
society, but there is usually some documentation for the
necessity for this step. The patient may have a reputation
for certain types of behavior. At least he has given someone sufficient cause for concern that he has gone beyond the
earlier steps that might be taken, such as referral for outpatient evaluation or treatment. Cause for alarm has been
communicated.

At the same time, on an inpatient service one is not
alone with the patient, and there is at least the ready
possibility of setting in motion mechanisms for protecting
the patient, other patients, and staff. It is, therefore,
a relatively protected environment. For some patients this
very fact may diminish their anxiety about their potential
for destructive action. Some may also have been separated
from the object of their rage or fear and experience some
relief as a result. In contrast, for other patients the
very fact of their admission may become the focus of their
anger, and the staff, as instruments of this decision, become the object of the anger. In some cases this represents
displacement onto a ready object. In others this anger is
also an expression of the patient's fear: at being forced
into continued proximity to many people and at his inability
to escape his anxiety by his usual methods, whether self-
medication with drugs, activity, withdrawal, or physical
flight or fight.

The actual meeting of the patient with the therapist is
an enormously complicated event. The patient comes into the
presence of a man or a woman. This person has a professional
identity: counselor, psychiatrist, nurse, psychologist,
social worker, and so forth. What has the patient's experience been with this category of people? What are his beliefs and fantasies about them? This person has a professional purpose of his own, a goal, in seeing the patient, and

it may or may not be consonant with the patient's initial
purpose or goal. Whether the patient is brought against
his will, strongly encouraged to come, or even comes voluntarily, the therapist is in a position of relative authority. He has it in his power to gratify or frustrate the
patient. He can be willing and able to help the patient with
what the patient sees as his dilemma; or he may be neither.
He may not see the dilemma in the same way the patient does,
and he may even persist in his opinion despite the patient's
efforts to convince him. If the patient is psychotic, he
may actually believe the therapist is someone else and may
or may not communicate this fact. Who might this third person be and how does the patient feel about him?

Clearly, not the least of these factors, and one of the
most obvious, is the sex of the therapist. Patients, like
anyone else, may share general societal notions about males
and females. In addition, their own subcultures and families
may hold particular attitudes toward the sexes. They have
also had specific experiences with each, beginning with
infancy and continuing while undergoing modification through
adolescence and adulthood. It has often been hypothesized
that patients who are violent have been frustrated in their
attempts to establish stable, affectionate relationships
early in life--that they have been unable to form appropriate
identifications and have thus been unable to develop necessary ego functions. Possibly, then, the fundamental issue
for them is the more generic one of trust and need for, but
helplessness to get, a close and caring relationship, as
well as fear of its consequences. It cannot be ignored that
these people have the bodies and biological instincts of
adults, and that they have had sex-specific experiences with
men and women. However, we must remember that we are dealing fundamentally with individuals who are functioning devel-
opmentally at a pregenital, undifferentiated stage. The complex interplay of these factors is sketched in the following
example.

A young male patient was admitted to a ward on which I
was the senior administrator and as such had relatively
little direct contact with patients. He carried the
diagnosis of manic-depressive illness and, when not
actively psychotic, his lifestyle was that of an antisocial personality, evinced by participation in minor
criminal activities and addiction to heroin. When he

was first admitted he was belligerent, assaultive, loud, and sullen. He had several physical altercations with male staff, particularly when they attempted to set limits or administer medication, but some struggles were initiated by him. When he was present at ward meetings which I attended but during which I was usually not active, he focused his attention on me. His attitude was friendly, even ingratiating, and he frequently complimented me on my appearance, exhorting everyone to obey me and saying I was a "lady," was "smart," knew what was right and wrong. He finally said that I reminded him of one of his teachers in elementary school who was strict but nice and taught him a lot. He even identified with me to the extent of saying that he had a pair of shoes just like mine (rather high-heeled gray sandals) which he admired inordinately. Thereafter, even during difficult episodes for him, he treated me with respect and, when generally hostile, displayed only mildly depressed affect in contacts with me. He was always pleased when he saw me wearing the "bad" shoes that seemed to form a special bond between us. Staff remarked on the degree of interest he showed in me—a comparatively large personal input on his part, considering that our contacts amounted to nothing more than an occasional "Hello, how are you?" on my part. In the meantime, his relationship with his male therapist was marked by ambivalent dependency on the patient's part and affectionate and sometimes slightly impatient attempts at investigation and limit-setting on the part of the therapist, who found him likeable but not very introspective and rather intractable. Although he often argued with his therapist, was very resistant to attempts to engage him in discussion around his problems, and was quite irregular in his attendance to therapy sessions, the patient always maintained that the therapist was "his only friend in the world," and he would always appeal to him in a childlike way when he was in trouble. Furthermore, having established these relationships, such as they were, he never had any more fights on the ward, to the great relief of the staff who had at first experienced him as a dangerous and violent man.

It is certainly impossible to analyze closely the complexities of this situation, since there is little data from the patient. This case does appear, however, to be an exam-

ple of a man with strong, ungratified infantile needs who
turned to a male for nurturance and for whom the fact that
I was a woman, gray-haired, and in a position of authority, had special, though obscure, meanings.

A sex-specific response in a primitive patient is exemplified in the following excerpt.

> A schizophrenic woman in her forties came from a hos-
> pital in another state where she had been institution-
> alized for many years with a history of having killed
> another female patient in a fight some years earlier.
> She was large, strong, and for the most part childlike,
> compliant, and eager to please. She would, however,
> occasionally fly into rages during which she would
> attack, and had consequently injured female staff, par-
> ticularly those with long blonde hair. Large numbers of
> male staff and a protracted struggle were required to
> subdue her. She let us know over time that she had a
> younger sister with long blonde hair of whom she was
> extremely jealous. Under certain circumstances the
> sight of such an individual, or of a young female child
> receiving attention from adults, would provoke in her an
> intense, dysphoric emotional reaction. The staff ad-
> dressed itself to helping her identify and communicate
> the onset of this state. They then developed a system
> in which she and, if necessary, the staff would insti-
> tute controls to prevent her acting on her destructive
> impulses. This method was meeting with considerable
> success when last I heard of her. No one had been hurt,
> although a considerable number of staff members met the
> requirements for attack, and the patient was beginning
> to feel some small measure of self-esteem and trust in
> herself and others.

Continuing relationships with dangerous, impulsive, and
particularly "unpredictable" people present yet other problems. It is not productive to lump all such individuals into
one category. Both the antisocial personality, who may not
tolerate interference with his wish to get what he wants
immediately, and the borderline personality or paranoid
patient, who can form a psychotic transference to the therapist, pose real threats to the therapist's safety. Each, however, has different modes of relating and each requires cor-
respondingly different modifications of treatment approach.

(It should be noted that the characteristic of "unpredicta-
bility," which is perhaps the most frightening of all,
diminishes with increasing familiarity with the patient and
consequent knowledge about what is going on in his life
inside and outside of therapy.) There is a large amount of
literature and disagreement about the ways to understand and
handle ongoing treatment and crises with any of these patients, and I will not pursue this subject here.

Regarding the sex of the therapist, my earlier statements about primitive lack of differentiation remain true.
Patients can form maternal transferences to male therapists
and paternal transferences to female therapists, and these
can change, or become mixed, or remain stable over time.
These role reversals may, however, prove difficult for the
therapist. For instance, a male therapist may have some
resistance to seeing himself as an important female figure
and vice versa. On a different level, women therapists may
be seen in a variety of female roles, each carrying implications for countertransference in the therapist. Female
therapists I have supervised, as well as myself, have been
seen in a variety of forms and roles: cold, rejecting, or
indifferent mothers; overprotective and intrusive mothers;
ambivalently held mothers who have died or left; warm and
loving grandmothers or other female members of the extended
family; rejecting or inadequate female lovers or wives; nurse-
maids who had been loved and lost; and so forth. The patient
in each case might be either male or female.

In either case, the arousal of sexual feelings in patient
or therapist might prove problematic. As has been mentioned,
these patients usually do have biologically mature bodies
and the potential for sexual activity, however it may be
motivated. My work with male and female residents and staff
leads me to believe that males are no more comfortable with
aggressive sexual approaches than are females. The same
questions come to mind: How can one respond and still remain
helpful to the patient? What are one's own feelings toward
the patient? Has one in any way unwittingly provoked a
sexual response in the patient? Differences are revealed
in the matter of force. Most males do not think they can
actually be raped, by a female at least (although the fantasies may be there). Females, on the other hand, are not
so sure, or at least feel that rape by a male patient is a
possibility. The distinction between fantasy and reality,

of course, again assumes importance, as with other manifestations of violence. To what extent is the female therapist
literally seen as a reflection of earlier important persons,
and to what extent is she less consciously seen as a reflection of such persons and more consciously viewed as a distinct individual with whom the patient strongly wishes to
have sexual contact? In either case, the question of whether
she may become the victim of these feelings does arise.

A word should be added about the pregnant therapist.
This phenomenon is becoming more common with the increasing
entrance of women into the work force. It is no longer
unusual to find a psychologist, physician, social worker,
nurse, or occupational therapist in almost any clinical setting well into her third trimester, that is, very obviously
pregnant. Having been in this situation several times myself, I know that it can introduce a large number of complications as well as interesting developments. Briefly, and
limiting myself to the subject of violence, the most immediate reaction on the part of both therapist and staff is to
protect the baby as well as the mother. The pregnant woman
is not supposed to and does not wish to place herself, and
particularly the infant, in jeopardy. Intrepid women may
become more cautious and tentative in relating to patients.
This sometimes necessitates special arrangements of schedules
and places where the woman will work. Such manipulations can
arouse negative reactions in colleagues and renewed conflict
in the woman, who had perhaps thought issues of dependency
and vulnerability had been settled. When such accommodations
are not feasible, the woman must make a choice between not
working and taking some risks. In several instances that I
have been able to observe, women who are accustomed to being
in possibly dangerous situations have continued to work.
They have met the situation as a rule by open display and discussion of their condition. This, of course, also exposes
the woman as a real sexual object, a realization which may
be uncomfortable for both therapist and patient. Detailed
reviews of the subject of the pregnant therapist have been
presented by Nadelson, Notman, Arons, and Feldman (1974),
Baum and Herring (1975), Berman (1975), and Lax (1969).

Whether real or fantasied, the fear of any sort of
violence tends to be most prominent when the therapist is in
some way isolated with the patient. This is meant both in
the physical sense (alone in an office, in an isolated part

of the building, after work, or at home) and in the psychological sense (when one is in the position of being or feeling totally responsible for the patient--the sole repository of his thoughts and feelings, especially in opposition to the rest of the world). The therapist alone in private practice, without benefit of the presence of other professional persons and unable even to discuss informally the problem he has, must be in the most vulnerable position in this regard.

It is almost impossible to treat violent patients adequately without some sense of security and support. One must be sure that one is as safe as possible and also that the patient is aware of this. It is under such circumstances that the most calm, rational, and effective handling of anticipated or actual violence can be observed. The therapist should have as much information as possible about the patient, about herself and himself, and about the supporting staff. The therapist must approach the patient as a helping professional and orient him to the identity and purpose of the professional role. Above all, the situation must be approached with humility rather than omnipotence, and the patient must be treated with respect.

In spite of recent interest in women and consequent social changes, differences remain in the ways that professional women are viewed by others and themselves as distinct from men. I have indicated some of the ways in which the experience of the female is different in quality from that of the male therapist. I have also pointed out some ways in which it is the same and also some ways in which the male therapist faces problems of an equal but opposite nature. On balance, I would conclude that it is of importance that each recognize the countertransference, transference, and reality problems peculiar to his or her own sexual identity as an initial step in gaining competence to deal with the violent impulsive patient.

References

Baum, O.E. and Herring, C. 1975. The pregnant psychotherapist in training: some preliminary findings and impressions. Am. J. Psychiat., 132:4.

Berman, E. 1975. Acting out as a response to the psychiatrist's pregnancy. J. Am. Med. Wom. Assoc., Vol. 30, No. 11.

Josephson, M. 1934. The Robber Barons. New York: Harcourt Brace and Co.

Lax, R.F. 1969. Some considerations about transference and countertransference manifestations evoked by the analyst's pregnancy. Int. J. Psychoanal., 50:363-372.

Levy, P. and Hartocollis, P. 1976. Nursing aides and patient violence. Am. J. Psychiat., 133:4.

Lion, J.R., Azcarate, C., Christopher, R., and Arana, J.D. 1974. A violence clinic. Md. State Med. J., 23:45-48.

Lion, J.R., Bach-Y-Rita, G., and Ervin, F.R. 1968. The self-referred violent patient. JAMA, 205:503-505.

Lion, J.R., Bach-Y-Rita, G., and Ervin, F.R. 1969. Violent patients in the emergency room. Am. J. Psychiat. 125:12.

Lion, J.R., Madden, D.J., and Christopher, R.L. 1976. A violence clinic: three years' experience. Am. J. Psychiat., 133:4.

Lion, J.R. and Pasternak, S.A. 1973. Countertransference reactions to violent patients. Am. J. Psychiat. 130:2, Feb.

Macdonald, J.M. 1967. Homicidal threats. Am. J. Psychiat., 124:4.

Menninger, R.W. and Modlin, H.C. 1971. Individual violence: prevention in the violence-threatening patient. In, J. Fawcett (Ed.), Dynamics of Violence, 71-78. Chicago: Am. Med. Assoc.

Nadelson, C., Notman, M., Arons, E., and Feldman, J. 1974. The pregnant therapist. Am. J. Psychiat., 131:10.

Offer, D., Marohn, R.C., and Ostrov, E. 1976. Violence among hospitalized delinquents. Arch. Gen. Psychiatry, 32.

Schwartz, M.S. and Shocklye, E.L. 1956. The Nurse and the Mental Patient: A Study in Interpersonal Relations. New York: Russell Sage Foundation.

Seiden, A.M. 1976. Overview: research on the psychology of women, I. Gender differences and sexual and reproductive life. Am. J. Psychiat., 133:9.

Seiden, A.M. 1976. Overview: research on the psychology of women, II. Women in families, work, and psychotherapy. Am. J. Psychiat., 133:10.

Sendi, I.B. and Blumgren, P.G. 1975. A comparative study of predictive criteria in the predisposition of homicidal adolescents. Am. J. Psychiat., 132:4.

Spiegel, R. 1967. Anger and acting out: marks of depres-
     sion. Am. J. Psychother., 21:597-607.
Tarachow, S. "Paranoia and Homicide." In, An Introduction
     to Psychotherapy, Ch. 19, 291-299. New York: Interna-
     tional Universities Press.
Tardiff, K.J. 1974. A survey of psychiatrists in Boston
     and their work with violent patients. Am. J. Psychiat.,
     131:9.
Tuason, V.B. 1971. The psychiatrist and the violent pa-
     tient. Dis. Nerv. Syst., 32:764-768.
Whitman, R.M., Armao, B.B., and Dent, O.B. 1976. Assault
     on the therapist. Am. J. Psychiat., 133:4.
Zitrin, A., Hordesty, A.S., Burdock, E.I., and Drossman, A.
     1976. Crime and violence among mental patients. Am.
     J. Psychiat., 133:2.

Suggested Reading

Adler, G. and Shapiro, L.N. 1973. Some difficulties in the
     treatment of the aggressive acting-out patient. Am. J.
     Psychother., 27:548-556.
Anthony, J. 1969. The reactions of adults to adolescents
     and their behavior. In, G. Caplan and S. Lebovici
     (Eds.), Adolescence: Psychosocial Perspectives, 54-78.
     New York: Basic Books, Inc.
American Psychiatric Association Task Force Report 8, July,
     1974. Clinical Aspects of the Violent Individual.
Bach-Y-Rita, G. 1974. Habitual violence and self-mutila-
     tion. Am. J. Psychiat., 131:9.
Bach-Y-Rita, G., Lion, J.R., Climent, C.E., and Ervin, F.R.
     1971. Episodic dyscontrol: a study of 130 violent pa-
     tients. Am. J. Psychiat., 127:11.
Bach-Y-Rita, G. and Veno, A. 1974. Habitual violence: a
     profile of 62 men. Am. J. Psychiat., 131:9.
Benedek, E.P. 1973. The fourth world of the pregnant thera-
     pist. J. Am. Med. Wom. Assoc., 28:365.
Borriello, J.F. 1973. Patients with acting-out character
     disorders. Am. J. Psychother., 27:4-14.
Carney, F.L. 1973. Three important factors in psychotherapy
     with criminal patients. Am. J. Psychother., 27:220-321.
Cocozza, J.J. and Steadman, H.J. 1974. Some refinements in
     the measurement and prediction of dangerous behavior.
     Am. J. Psychiat., 131:9.

Duncan, J.W. and Duncan, G.M. 1971. Murder in the family: study of some homicidal adolescents. Am. J. Psychiat., 127:11.

Fromm-Reichman, F. 1952. The psychiatrist's part in the doctor-patient relationship. In, Principles of Intensive Psychotherpay, Ch. 2. Chicago: University of Chicago Press.

Hagen, D.Q., Mikolajczak, J., and Wright, R. 1972. Aggression in psychiatric patients. Comprehensive Psychiat., Vol. 13, No. 5.

Hartocollis, P. 1972. Aggressive behavior and the fear of violence. Adolescence, 7(28):479.

Kalogerakis, M.G. 1971. The assaultive psychiatric patient. Psychoanal. Q., 45:372-381.

Kozol, H.L., Boucher, R.J., and Garofalo, R.F. 1972. The diagnosis and treatment of dangerousness. Crime and Delinquency, 18:371-392.

Lion, J.R. 1972. Evaluation and Management of the Violent Patient. Springfield, Ill.: Charles C Thomas.

Lion, J.R. 1972. The role of depression in the treatment of aggressive personality disorders. Am. J. Psychiat., 129:3.

Lion, J.R. and Bach-Y-Rita, G. 1970. Group therapy with violent outpatients. Int. J. Group Psychother., 20:185-191.

Lion, J.R. and Leaff, L.A. 1973. On the hazards of assessing character pathology in an outpatient setting: a brief clinical note. Psychoanal. Q., 42:104-109.

Lion, J.R., Levenberg, L.B., and Strange, R.E. 1972. Restraining the violent patient. J. Psych. Nurs., 10(2):9-11.

Macdonald, J.M. 1966. The prompt diagnosis of psychopathic personality. Am. J. Psychiat., 122(June Suppl.):45-50.

Maddon, D.J., Lion, J.R., and Penna, M.W. 1976. Assaults on psychiatrists by patients. Am. J. Psychiat., 133:4.

Offer, D. 1971. Coping with aggression among normal adolescent males. In, J. Fawcett (Ed.), Dynamics of Violence, 171-185. Chicago: Am. Med. Assn.

ENGAGING THE IMPULSIVE PATIENT IN PSYCHOTHERAPY

Henry J. Friedman, M.D.

Associate Professor of Psychiatry and Director,
Outpatient Psychiatry, New England Medical Center
Hospital, Boston, Massachusetts

Although the scope of analytic psychotherapy has broadened over the past twenty years to include patients with
impulsive disorders, this enlarged treatment focus has occurred without a technical or theoretical framework to guide
innovative techniques. The concept of impulsivity as a character trait and/or symptom is broad and includes a range of
disorders. While it is important to make distinctions among
the different types of clinical disorders, I shall use in
this paper a more general definition of impulsivity, namely:
those behaviors which occur under emotional stress and result
in a negative impact upon the individual or those around him.
In chronically impulsive individuals, however, certain behavioral patterns can become autonomous, distinct from the
emotional pressures that were their point of origin. In
such patients, impulsive behavior may continue to occupy
their lives to such an extent that both the development and
consequent substitution of sublimating activities is obviated.

It is well known that Freud began his work with patients
suffering from symptomatology which was the inverse of impulsive activity. Whether it was a matter of case selection
or of the social milieu of the times, issues of impulsive
behavior were far less important to Freud in his initial
practice of psychoanalysis than to subsequent therapists
with an analytic orientation. In fact, one would assume from

early Freudian techniques that impulsive behavior was hardly
within the realm of the psychoanalyst's work. August Aichhorn's psychoanalytically based work with delinquent youth
in Vienna during the 1920s (1935) indicates, however, that
Freud's interest in behavioral disturbances was present, even
though he delegated this work to other individuals.

In working with delinquent youth the importance of the
therapist's personality as a factor in establishing therapeutic rapport has long been stressed. Eissler (1948) and
Friedlander (1960) both have viewed the analyst's personality
as one of the crucial factors in the establishment of a
therapeutic relationship with delinquent individuals. The
importance of the therapist's personality has been stressed
by Claude Brown, an ex-delinquent who is now a lawyer. In
his autobiography, Manchild in the Promised Land, he describes
the impact of personal encounters with important individuals
who "reached" him and influenced him to turn away from delinquency. It is not surprising, however, that full analytic
or even psychoanalytic psychotherapy of delinquent individuals
has not been reported with any great frequency. Few individuals with this type of manifest behavior are in a position to sustain the arrangements of intensive psychotherapy.
Furthermore, the results of therapeutic efforts conducted
within the confines of penal institutions often leave more
questions unanswered than problems solved.

Despite some apparent changes in social standards, most
of us within the field continue to consider impulsive behavior as well as impulsive character traits undesirable.
Impulsivity may be reflected in mental as well as motoric and
behavioral functioning. Impulsive traits, such as jumping
to conclusions with inadequate evidence, or responding to
parts of a situation or a person as if they were the whole,
are all aspects of neurosis encountered routinely in individual analytically oriented psychotherapy. It would, in fact,
be an unusual patient--or human being--who manifest none of
these impulsive traits. Chronically and persistently impulsive personalities, however, introduce difficulties of a
greater magnitude and also present a different set of problems for the psychotherapist.

Although practitioners of intensive psychotherapy in
outpatient settings have limited experience with grossly
impulsive individuals, under certain circumstances treatment

of these patients can be initiated which aims, over the course
of time, at modification of the impulse disorder.

Classification of Impulse Disorders and Problems

To label a person or action as impulsive almost uniformly connotes a negative judgment or evaluation. When
dealing with neurotic illness, it is possible to view the
therapeutic-analytic task as one of decreasing the dominance
of unconscious conflicts in manifest behavior. The result
of this task, if successfully accomplished, is to decrease
activities which are often impulsive in the sense that they
do not take into account all the factors (particularly unconscious ones) pertinent to a situation or interpersonal
relationship. Grossly impulsive behavior, however, is not
subtle and is hence easily identifiable. These patterns of
behavior tend to recur as more than isolated episodes,
and they involve areas of pleasure and/or escape from pain,
whether emanating from boredom or unacknowledged stress.
Delinquency has already been noted as a special form of impulsive behavior. Impulsive activity usually occurs in the
areas of eating, drinking, drug usage, sexuality, sudden
shifts in interpersonal relationships, job inconsistency,
and truancy.

For clinical purposes, impulsive behavior is most effectively assessed by the degree of conflict within the total
character structure regarding the particular actions involved.
Treatability is often determined on the basis of this assessment. This is not to imply that the absence of conflict
concerning impulsive behavior or character traits precludes
the possibility for psychotherapeutic intervention. However, the degree of conflict does influence, to a significant extent, what technical measures will be helpful in the
treatment of such patients.

In my experience, those cases where gross impulsive
behavior has become incorporated into the ego structure of
the individual require a technique distinctly different from
that suitable for psychoanalysis or psychoanalytic psychotherapy of neurotic individuals with some impulsive traits.
Although this technique requires that the therapist have a
high degree of psychodynamic understanding, he must alter his
approach and become more verbally and emotionally available
for interaction. This does not mean that the therapist be-

comes involved in unstructured "supportive" or "relationship
therapy." It does, however, require that the "fit" of the
therapist's and the patient's personalities is such that a
basically positive, even idealizing, transference results.

Although impulsive antisocial behavior has frequently
been linked to superego defect, less has been written about
deficiences in ego-ideal formation within the superego. Dis-
regard for morality, rather than apparent lack of positive,
shared standards and life values, has been stressed by many
psychoanalytically oriented therapists. The importance of
this distinction becomes crucial in distinguishing those impulsive individuals who can be worked with in psychotherapy
from those who may not only defy being worked with but may
be dangerous to treat. It is not always possible to make
this distinction rapidly, and, in fact, it may emerge only
through clinical experience with a variety of patients over
a long period of time.

Freud's early clinical observation that both analysands
and analysts must share a more or less similar set of values
(these often being the ethical, goal-oriented views of life
shared by the majority of individuals in the society) is a
dictum often ignored in the treatment of impulse-ridden patients. This is particularly unfortunate because the success
or failure of treatment with such individuals often rests
on the ability of the therapist to work with patients who do
not share similar values and, in part, to convey a new set
of values to them.

Although classification of the source of the impulsive
behavior in relation to developmental failure is possible and
may be helpful to the patient, it is not essential for achieving a change in behavior. Difficulties with regard to locat-
ing and accepting the source of the problem by the patient has
been addressed from the beginning of dynamic analytic work
within the context of "resistance." The narrowness of this
approach was recognized by Zetzel (1971) when she introduced
the concept of the therapeutic alliance. In neurotic patients
this alliance develops almost automatically with little
effort on the therapist's part. In patients with character
disorders, however, it does not develop without considerable
activity from the therapist. Resistances involving absence
of normative values in a patient may be approached through
attempts to establish a therapeutic alliance. Greenson (1967)

proposed substituting the term "working alliance" for "therapeutic alliance" because he felt it acknowledged the two-party nature of the treatment process, emphasizing the active part that both patient and therapist play in forming such an alliance. To illustrate I will describe two clinical cases in which both patients were extremely disturbed, impulsive, nonpsychotic individuals whose impulsive behavior persisted without any conscious wish on their part to alter it or gain insight into its meaning.

Case I

Fran S. was referred for psychotherapy at age 17 through the intervention of the mother's therapist. The mother had been seen in supportive psychotherapy for many years concerning chronic family problems and her own paranoid personality. Mrs. S.'s major deficiencies in empathic understanding and relating were reflected in a family filled with disorders, including the suicide of Fran's older sister at the age of 19, when Fran was 11 years old. This sister, who from description appears to have suffered both characterological and psychotic disorders, had dominated the family for many years prior to her suicide with her multiple institutionalizations, hyperaggressivity, and violent personality. Two older brothers seemed of relatively lesser importance to the patient; both, however, had managed to make only marginal adjustments in their lives.

The patient had a history of numerous previous attempts at psychotherapy, ranging from individual treatment to multiple-family group psychotherapy. All of these interventions were viewed by her as basically worthless, and she had a markedly negative but colorful view of a variety of psychotherapists in the large urban area where she lived. There was some evidence that previous psychotherapeutic interventions might have contributed to Fran's maladjusted behavior by encouraging her to leave her home and join a variety of informal living arrangements, foster homes, and nonacademic, alternative education schooling environments. During these placements she began her involvement with a variety of young homosexual men who became the center of her social life. With these individuals she partied continually, lived a totally disorganized life, and took enormous amounts of drugs and alcohol. Although she was artistically

talented and extremely interested in painting, her disorganized life style permitted very little actual work. At the
time of the initial referral, very little of this history
was known to me. In fact, had I been familiar with the details of her life, I would have been quite dubious about
accepting such a referral for private individual treatment.

In the first interview the patient appeared as she would
more or less continue to appear--an eccentric, peculiarly
dressed young woman with a tough exterior that ran quite
deep. Her cynicism was remarkable. From the start it was
clear that in her past treatment she had concentrated more
on denigrating her therapists than on understanding herself.
Although I did not feel that she was in any way a frightening individual in terms of being potentially violent or truly
suicidal, I did feel that engaging this patient in a treatment relationship would be more or less impossible. I knew
that she had seen competent psychiatrists in the past and
had maintained a steadfastly negative feeling toward all of
them. I also knew that her ability to tolerate a formal,
analytic type of technique, with emphasis on free communication and insight, was unlikely, considering the nature of
her psychopathology and her age.

Since this is a case in which a greater degree of engagement occurred than was originally anticipated, it may be
useful to describe the nature of the initial interview. It
was characterized by a good deal of relaxed conversation concerning the paintings, drawings, and furnishings in the office. Fran brought up the questions on these matters and I
responded to her curiosity. Under other circumstances, rather than participating in such a discussion, I would have
asked the patient about the reasons for the questions. However, in helping to present an altered ego ideal for such
patients, it may be helpful to join in such discussion, while
being cautious not to burden the patient with details of
one's personal experience beyond that encompassed by immediate responses. At the end of the first interview I asked
Fran if she would not ultimately find me as insufficient as
her previous psychiatrists. Although she was unwilling to
discuss the matter, she insisted that this was not likely
to be the case. I did not share my concern about this with
her any further and accepted her eagerness for a subsequent
appointment as sufficient grounds to continue, for the time
being.

During the early months of treatment the impulse-ridden nature of Fran's life became clearer. Through the use of a combination of quaaludes and alcohol, she would frequently reach a stuperous state during which she would often hit her head and become unconscious for varying periods of time. In addition, she was involved with a variety of individuals from homosexual and transsexual subcommunities and was intermittently functioning as a prostitute under extremely dangerous conditions. Most important in regard to consideration of impulsive personality disorders was the fact that neither the danger nor the self-destructiveness of her activities appeared to concern her in the least. Although she had said in the initial visit that she wanted help for feeling chronically anxious and bad, none of the impulsive behavior was seen as connected with her bad feelings. She insisted that this behavior was an alternative life style which, she claimed, I simply couldn't understand.

From the onset of treatment, I had extremely low expectations for achieving the usual goals of insight-oriented psychotherapy because of the patient's lack of interest in understanding herself. The situation, however, was not without some positive factors. Fran seemed to be extremely eager to see me. She had a good sense of humor and a strong wish to be admired by somebody she felt was interesting and worthwhile. For my part, I felt that any confrontation or attention to her resistance to analyzing would be futile. In the first several months of treatment, however, two confrontations were extremely important to the subsequent treatment course. The first occurred when the fact emerged that the patient was working as a prostitute to earn money for drugs and to lend her friends. I told her that this activity was incompatible with any kind of psychotherapy. She was placing herself in great danger and I could not help her if she was murdered in the course of her impulsive pursuits. She did not agree with me regarding the extent of the danger, but she did agree to stop it in order to continue treatment. The second confrontation focused on her excessive use of alcohol and quaaludes. She agreed to limit her consumption if she was given an antianxiety agent. I reluctantly agreed to this trade-off.

Fran has been in once-weekly psychotherapy for the past four years. The treatment can be characterized as conversational, lively, and nonassociative. She talks a great deal about her life and the people in it. Her intense sexual-

ity is a matter of great pride to her and she is in constant
pursuit of all-consuming relationships which she finds and
exhausts in surprisingly short periods of time. Both men
and women are the objects of these relationships but her
preference is for women. She no longer uses drugs, her alcohol consumption has markedly decreased, she is close to
completing an undergraduate degree, and in general lives in
a much more disciplined and less self-destructive fashion.
An associative technique remains inappropriate for her treatment, and her homosexuality and impulsivity in relationships
are still not considered subjects for the treatment insofar
as she is concerned. However, the influence of the treatment relationship on this patient's life became clear when
she responded to my questioning its value by reminding me,
with great indignation, that without treatment she would
still be taking quaaludes and "hooking." Therapeutic goals
had in fact been reached but they were derived through behavior change rather than verbally defined insight.

Discussion

This case is presented as an example of the successful
treatment of an impulse-ridden individual with little serious
evidence of conflict over impulsive behavior or its consequences. From a traditional framework, with patients like
Fran, three features of the therapy are most striking: absence of a therapeutic alliance, lack of insight as the means
of behavioral change, and an essential lack of focus for the
treatment. In working with such patients the therapist may
have to accept that progress does not mean absence of major
pathology. Three primary factors comprise a telling difference in therapeutic technique employed with this patient:
(1) the transference is allowed (encouraged) to stabilize in
a positive configuration and is not analyzed with the patient; (2) limits are set through this transference (but only
when they are essential to the patient's survival and within
his or her ability to cope; (3) constant awareness of the patient's coping ability. These factors coalesced in the management of Fran's Valium dependency. For although such a
dependency is not desirable, it is far less destructive than
her dependency on quaaludes and alcohol. Initially, she could
not cope without some substance. As the positive transference developed over a course of three years, she gave up
Valium.

An essential factor in the treatment of people with impulsive character disorders is the ability of the therapist to share his ego and superego capacities in order to lessen these deficiences in the patient, and is dependent upon the existence of an essentially positive transference relationship. Although Fran's identification may have been based on her narcissism, it nonetheless became the foundation upon which she could be moved toward a healthier life with fewer gross impulsive actions. The absence of these actions allowed her to develop a semblance of a positive ego ideal and actually make some progress toward its realization.

While I would agree with the usual clinical reservation about the possibility of changing chronic, long-term impulsive behavior patterns, it is essential to remain aware of exceptions and recognize that with appropriate psychotherapeutic techniques, including considerable manipulation of the transference which psychotherapy permits, changes can occur even in those situations that appear least promising. To further illustrate the degree of change possible, I will present part of the history and treatment of an individual with a high degree of behavioral regression with whom a striking reversal was achieved through a relatively brief (year-and-a-half) period of psychotherapeutic intervention.

Case II

Mr. S. experienced a slow but progressive regression that was complicated by his heavy drug usage. Although the patient could acknowledge the self-destructiveness of his lifestyle, he could do little to control it, and for a long period of time, differentiation between slow progress and no progress was extremely difficult. Mr. S. first sought treatment in the midst of a tumultuous fight with his father. The patient felt (with considerable support from his description) that his father was a stubborn, narcissistic, domineering man who insisted, both overtly and covertly, that his own particular lifestyle take precedence over the needs of others in the family. The patient was particularly infuriated because his mother, a woman with an intense masochistic orientation toward her husband, refused to acknowledge his insensitivity and narcissistic nature. Instead, she attempted to placate the patient by denying the effects of the father's behavior. At the time the patient first sought treatment, his previous impulsive behavior had re-

sulted in his becoming dependent upon his father for financial support. He worked as a laborer in his father's small
manufacturing business, and although the father paid his son
a magnificent salary for his work, he would in no way allow
him to have any administrative responsibility or decision-
making input in the business. The father was willing to
pay the inflated salary if his son accepted all his dicta
about how to live his life both during and after work. The
patient accepted these directives for several months, but
friction developed over petty differences in day-to-day contact. The central theme had remained the same since early
in his childhood: whenever the patient found evidence of his
father's indifference--whether manifest as not spending time
with him as a child or lack of interest in a grown son's
views on the business--he would become explosively angry and
get into a violent argument with him. When a fight erupted,
the father would withdraw into silence, the patient would
walk out, and the mother would take to her bed and blame her
symptoms on the conflict between the two. A sister two
years older, married, and out of the home would often rein-
force the mother's pleas for a reconciliation between father
and son. The patient's father had broken with his own father
with whom he had not talked for years and with whom he had
not been able to reconcile himself even when death was im-
minent.

    The patient clearly was not one who easily sought or
utilized individual psychotherapy. If he had been, he would
have sought aid much earlier after recognizing his acute
distress. Despite the chronic family imbalance and irration-
ality, the patient had managed to negotiate basic developmental steps. He had never been an outstanding student nor
had he felt any real satisfactions in most of his activities.
A great deal of energy always seemed to be directed at his
father--as if he was keeping track of the father's apparent
lack of satisfaction or interest in him. (This in fact could
have been central to his lack of scholastic achievement, as
he certainly appeared to be adequately endowed intellec-
tually.) He did manage to finish an undergraduate degree
and began work as an insurance salesman. Initially he was
moderately successful at this work but felt, retrospectively,
that this was due to the use of parental contacts. He met
and married a woman whom he appeared to know only superfi-
cially but was in part attracted to because of her wealthy
and successful father, who held out promises of future busi-

ness associations and success. But the patient's marriage and business life deteriorated simultaneously; at about the same time that he and his wife split up, he became increasingly disillusioned with selling insurance. He felt that he was attempting to please authority figures at work while engaging in what he considered to be basically a dishonest business.

When he began treatment he had already spent three years during which he had been mostly unemployed. Sporadic efforts at work involved close friends who themselves were tied to family businesses and could only offer him low-paying jobs that held little hope for the future. The patient was spending large amounts of time sleeping or taking marijuana. He had practically no contact with any friends or relatives and was profoundly cynical and angry at what he correctly saw as the insensitivity of certain of his friends. What he could not do was to make progressive changes and attempt to bring any new people into his life.

The patient at age 27 seemed to have no options remaining for him (from his point of view) in either the personal or work spheres of his life. Because he had given up trying in all major areas of his life, his positive motivation for psychotherapy seemed incompatible with his pessimistic attitude and situation. It was therefore surprising when he formed a strong initial therapeutic alliance based on his feeling that the therapist understood that his father was a very disordered individual. Clarification and insight regarding this permitted him to accept his own excessive involvement in fighting with his father as a part of the problem, and from early in treatment the patient was able to work on understanding the family dynamics. This increased understanding did not, however, relieve the struggle with the father, who eventually fired him and left him without a source of income.

Although the patient continued to attend psychotherapeutic sessions regularly, he retreated into his apartment and began using marijuana. He saw the drug usage as a crutch but was not willing or able to make active efforts to stop its use. Presence of insight accompanied by continued behavioral disturbance is usually viewed as a negative prognostic sign. And this patient realized the destructiveness of his drug dependency but maintained his need for treatment

while remaining refractory about his drug use. He did not
want to give up the treatment because, in his words, it
represented the only source of hope that he had had in years.
Of this he was both conscious and insistent.

He required continual encouragement not to give up on
his life but to continue making efforts in both the work and
personal spheres. Just as it appeared that no change what-
soever was possible, the patient found a job in real estate
management. He had a persistent fantasy that his hard work
(he did in fact work very hard) would be rewarded by advance-
ment. In fact, from what he had said about his employer,
this seemed highly unlikely, and he had to be helped to
recognize the limitations of this job. I viewed the job as
a temporary situation that served to keep the patient both
economically solvent and out of his apartment at least nine
hours a day. When the patient began working and also having
some minimal social life, his drug usage decreased or ceased
entirely.

Discussion

Throughout the course of treatment Mr. S. maintained a
positive but not idealizing attitude toward me. He was particularly surprised by any insight that increased his understanding of either himself or the few figures in his life.
It was particularly helpful to him to realize that his
mother's continual complaint that he did not come to see her
completely ignored her own lack of reaching out to him and
her basic dedication to the patient's father as her primary
obligation in life. One of the ways in which my own activity
in this treatment was different than usual involved the patient's decision to leave the area and move to another city
where possible business opportunities were greater. This
occurred when the patient received an offer from a friend to
start a wholesale business on the West coast. The patient,
despite years of hope for some opportunity like this, felt
entirely paralyzed and unable to leave. At this time he
appeared much more phobic and limited in his scope of activity
than I had supposed. I pointed out that this opportunity had
been a long time in coming and he couldn't turn it down out
of negativism or unfounded fear. Despite his doubts and
fears, he decided to move and try his luck in a new situation.
A six-month followup revealed that Mr. S. was able to relocate
away from his parents and start a new business and personal

life. No resumption of heavy drug usage has occurred despite
the fact that his new life requires long and hard hours of
work under stressful conditions.

Conclusion

Problems of engagement and its relation to changes in
treatment style have not always been given sufficient attention in the psychoanalytic literature. While the psychodynamics of resistance can deal with serious impediments to
meaningful engagement in treatment, efforts to involve patients actively have tended to be viewed as manipulative and
hence not within the framework of analytic psychotherapy.
Modell (1977), for example, has pointed to the protective
"cocoon state" that appears in the treatment of narcissistic
personalities and persists for as long as a year before real
engagement between analyst and analysand can occur. Greenson (1967), in contrast, has used vivid clinical examples
to illustrate that failures in treatment may result from an
excessively rigid psychoanalytic technique, as well as mistakes in diagnostic assessment.

Despite the fact that authors have to varying extents
suggested loosening some of the traditional strictures of
psychoanalytic technique, they nonetheless adhere to requirements for both analyst and analysand that rely strongly on
traditional precepts. Both Modell and Greenson describe the
treatment situation as placing limitations on the kind of
participation required of each party; and both focus on the
quality of associative material and accompanying affects in
a four-to-five times weekly regimen with patients who seek
and are able to use insight-based treatment. Greenson's case
examples involve patients who were experiencing second and
third analyses and for whom the inflexibility of previous
techniques had interfered with their use of treatment to a
serious extent. These patients, like those described in this
paper, required a more active technique. But, unlike Greenson's patients, those presented here were unable to form a
working alliance around an insight-oriented treatment goal.
Rather, they responded through an attachment to the therapist, for whom they appeared to alter some of their behavioral disturbances.

The purpose of presenting these cases is to illustrate
the fact that therapeutic work can be accomplished within a

framework that accepts the possibility of limited therapeutic
goals for certain patients. Therapeutic changes do not follow in these cases from a systematic examination of all
neurotic elements in the patient's life with an emphasis on
their genetic origins. Patients in this group appear to
benefit greatly from a positive relationship with the therapist, and in this context they may even be willing to accept
an insight approach, particularly in areas that do not involve reward-punishment mechanisms to any great extent. In
this area these patients will most probably retain disturbed
behavior patterns which they continue to see as perfectly
compatible with their internal standards of normal and acceptable functioning.

Both patients described here gave up certain impulsive
behavioral responses without acknowledging a conflict over
those behaviors. But the overall changes in their lives
were significant to them both subjectively and objectively;
both individuals were far less regressed than prior to
treatment. In terms of understanding the impact of therapy
on these two patients, I view the positive relationship with
the therapist as having provided the possibility for influ-
encing a more constructive direction for their lives. The
importance of such changes in traditional psychoanalytically
oriented psychotherapies may be underestimated because of
our tendency to concentrate exclusively on insight and ignore
other healing aspects of the therapeutic relationship.

A major task confronting professionals who practice
dynamically based psychotherapy with a wide variety of patients is the ability and willingness to make an important
distinction among them--to differentiate those, on the one
hand, with significant and unusual resistances to treatment,
who are nonetheless able to make use of therapeutic interventions, from those, on the other, whose antagonistic attitudes, opinions, and behaviors are incompatible with psycho-
therapeutically based change. This latter group of patients
are refractory to dynamically based clinical intervention.

This paper has reviewed some of the treatment problems
with a category of patients often viewed as having a poor
prognosis for successful psychotherapeutic intervention--
namely, impulsive personalities with minimal amounts of overt
conflict concerning their behavior patterns, as well as minimal regard for the processes of reflection, contemplation,

analysis, and insight--qualities usually considered crucial
criteria for treatability in analytic psychotherapy.

The case material presented emphasizes the use of the
therapeutic relationship--particularly its positive aspects--
to influence the degree of pathological behavior expressed
in action. Establishing a positive therapeutic relationship,
which can be utilized to promote the control of impulsive
behavior, is highlighted as a central criterion for treatability of impulsive personalities.

References

Aichhorn, A. 1935. Wayward Youth. New York: Viking Press.
Brown, C. 1965. Manchild in the Promised Land. New York:
    Macmillan.
Eissler, K. 1948. Searchlight on Delinquency. New York:
    International Universities Press.
Friedlander, K. 1960. The Psychoanalytical Approach to
    Juvenile Delinquency Theory, Case Studies, Treatment.
    New York: International Universities Press Inc.
Greenson, R. 1967. The Technique and Practice of Psycho-
    analysis. Vol. 1. New York: International Universities
    Press.
Modell, A. 1977. Presentation at Winter Meeting of the
    American Psychoanalytic Association. Panel on the Nature
    of Change in Psychoanalysis.
Zetzel, E. 1971. The Capacity for Emotional Growth. New
    York: International Universities Press.

IMPULSE PROBLEMS AND DRUG ADDICTION: CAUSE

AND EFFECT RELATIONSHIPS

Edward J. Khantzian, M.D.

Associate Director, Department of Psychiatry,
The Cambridge Hospital, and Associate Professor
of Psychiatry, Harvard Medical School at The
Cambridge Hospital, Cambridge, Massachusetts

The aim of this paper is to explore some of the important interrelationships of drug use/dependency and impulse
problems. Over the past fifteen years mental health professionals and citizens alike have been inundated by accounts
in the mass media and in the scientific literature that link
drug use/dependency with criminality, violence, brutality,
and other forms of antisocial behavior. Not infrequently,
the characterizations and accounts of such cases blur the
links between the drugs and the disturbed behavior, and the
consequent suggested or implied relationship between the two
is overdrawn, stereotyped, and/or unspecified. This discussion attempts to specify some of the relationships between
impulse problems and drugs, placing a particular emphasis
on problems with aggression. Drawing upon clinical examples,
I will attempt to show how the specific psychopharmacologic
actions of the three main classes of drugs upon which individuals become dependent--stimulants, sedatives/hypnotics,
and opiates--interact with personality and other emotional
factors, and how this interaction may affect behavior.

Background and Overview

Early psychiatric and psychoanalytic literature on addiction emphasizes the pleasurable and regressive aspects of
drug use in accounting for why people become dependent on

drugs (Khantzian, 1974). Rado (1933), an American psychoanalyst who pioneered in exploring the psychodynamics of
drug use, strongly influenced this trend in his early writings
on drug dependence. Although he seemed to appreciate underlying factors of depression, he unduly emphasized the "he-
donic" interests of the addict and the seeking of a "super-
pleasure" to explain the compelling nature of addiction.
Over the subsequent quarter century, other investigators
and social commentators have repeatedly cited and concurred
with Rado's findings, and popular street terms reflect this
emphasis in describing the drug experience--"high," "getting
off," "cheap thrills," and so forth. It is little wonder then
that we are quick to associate drug dependency with "pleasure-
seekers," irresponsibility, and impulsivity.

In contrast to early emphasis on gratification of in-
stinctual impulses, subsequent investigators (Chein, et al.,
1964; Weider and Kaplan, 1969; Krystal and Raskin, 1970;
Khantzian, 1974; Wurmser, 1974) placed greater emphasis on
problems of impulse control and regulation, affect tolerance,
and management of drives in drug-dependent people. These
reports stress an adaptive use of drugs wherein individuals,
in lieu of adequate defenses and impaired ego capacities,
adopt the use of drugs in the service of drive and affect
defense (Wurmser, 1974; Khantzian, 1974) or to augment and/or
facilitate certain desired ego states (Weider and Kaplan,
1969). In simpler and less technical terms, these latter
formulations suggest that drug dependency has less to do with
pleasure-seeking than with an individual's boundaries and
defenses regarding both internal feelings and the external
world.

The addict suffers immensely with his feelings, drives,
and relationships with other people. His boundaries (Wurmser, 1977) and ego defense mechanisms are either rigidly
overdrawn and painfully limiting, or they are alarmingly
brittle or absent (Kohut, 1971). In other cases they are
only poorly developed and barely adequate for negotiating
any challenge or satisfaction. At other times the addict's
boundaries and defenses play even crueler tricks on him,
resulting in rapid, unpredictable, and seemingly unmanage-
able shifts: he either feels too much or not enough. It
is in response to this state of affairs within different drug-
dependent individuals, or at different points in time within
the same individual, that various drugs take on such a com-

pelling quality. Most addicts take drugs to compensate for developmental impairments in the ego. They augment shaky or absent defenses with a particular drug, or take advantage of a drug effect to produce certain feelings, actions, or activities for which they otherwise feel incapable.

It is also from this state of affairs that some of the cause-and-effect relationships between drugs and impulsive behavior develop. Some individuals become addicted to drugs because of an inability to cope with particular feelings; without the drug they are subject to overwhelming affects and impulses that seem intolerable. In other instances, drugs permit individuals to overcome sufficient inhibitions and barriers against interpersonal involvement, often related to fear of impulses, to allow them to seek out (possibly for the first time) some semblance of human contact and involvement with work and play. This defensive or facilitating use of drugs to deal with powerful affects that might lead to impulsive acts, or to liberate individuals from fears of impulsivity, illustrates the "cause" aspect of drug-dependency problems. In other instances, drug-dependent people, as a result of drug use, display massive rage and anger, bizarre and totally inappropriate behavior, or significant pathological withdrawal and regression. These latter examples of extreme behavior reflect the "effect" aspect of drug abuse.

Fortunately, and in most instances, the examples of drug dependency that follow are not as apparent, extreme, or problematic; rather, they range along a continuum. In the majority of cases, the desired effect produces "an altered state of consciousness" in order to enhance control, facilitate performance, or relieve distress. Only rarely is behavior affected to an extreme. But it is in these extreme instances that drug dependence leads to alarming, dramatic impulses and behavior, and becomes the focus of grave concern.

I will attempt to delineate the continuum of drug effects and reactions in relation to stimulants, sedatives/hypnotics, and opiates, and to spell out some of the adaptive and maladaptive results of using such drugs. With a focus on impulsivity, I will emphasize issues of aggression and control, that is, how in certain instances these drugs support and enhance control of impulses and aggression, while in others they undermine or abolish controls, leading to impulsive and destructive behavior.

Interrelation of Impulsivity and Drug Groups

Previous reports (Weider and Kaplan, 1969; Milkman and
Frosch, 1973; Khantzian, 1975) have stressed the fact that
despite experimentation with a variety of drugs, individuals
tend to self-select and have particular preferences. This
predilection for particular drugs is in many cases based on
the "fit" of an individual's personality structure, including
his reactive patterns, with the distinctive psychopharmacologic action of the drug of choice. In most instances, the appeal of drugs rests on this specific interrelation, wherein
the drug helps to relieve internal dysphoric and distressful
states and/or leads to improved function. The following
descriptions and clinical examples illustrate some of the
interrelations of impulse problems and the three main categories of drugs that are misused.

Stimulants

Amphetamines and cocaine are the two main drugs in the
stimulant category and share an energizing or drive-augment-
ing action. For many, these drugs are appealing because they
assist in overcoming fatigue and depletion states associated
with depression. Wurmser (1974) states that they help to
overcome depression by inducing a sense of "aggression mastery, control, invincibility and grandiosity." In my own
clinical experience, I have been repeatedly impressed by how
the use of these drugs became compelling for certain people
as they discovered they were able to accomplish chores and
overcome various tasks for which they previously felt incapable. The following case excerpt illustrates this nicely.

> A 25-year-old separated mother of two young children
> described an impoverished, lonely existence in which she
> cared for her children in a two-room flat in a congested,
> low-income neighborhood. Residence in this particular
> neighborhood had in part been chosen because of her hus-
> band's ethnic background. When he abandoned her, her
> distressful feelings of estrangement and loneliness were
> compounded by the isolation she experienced in a com-
> munity whose cultural and ethnic traditions were alien
> to her. A friend introduced her to methamphetamine
> (which she initially took orally). She experienced a
> surge of energy that resulted in a frenetic, welcome

burst of enthusiasm to clean up her flat. The dishev-
elled state of the apartment resulted from and further
compounded a depression she only vaguely perceived.
As she repeatedly tried to recapture feelings of new-
found energy and the elation of being able to complete
some tasks, she required larger doses, including intra-
venous use. This soon led to a two-year binge of protracted "amphetamine runs" that resulted in the personal
and physical deterioration accompanying major physio-
logic dependence.

Many drug-dependent individuals have enormous difficulty
in identifying and tolerating painful emotional states, particularly depression (Krystal and Raskin, 1970). The foregoing clinical excerpt is not atypical of a person who only
dimly perceives his or her depression, despite overwhelming
subjective and external reality factors that would dispose
one to this state. Physiologically, the drug presumably
mobilizes and energizes the patient by acting on catecholamine
metabolism and release of norepinephrine in certain central
nervous system receptor sites (Schildkraut, 1965). In my
opinion, we often misidentify the directions of neurochemical
change: what may be the chemical transformation of depressive anergia and dysphoria to elation and hyperactivity is
perceived as the "high" or euphoria obtained with stimulants.

Weider and Kaplan (1969) posit a somewhat different
basis on which individuals use and become dependent on stimulants. They have observed that amphetamines enhance feelings of mastery and activity, resulting in greater assertive-
ness, self-esteem, and frustration tolerance. This is congruent with my own clinical observations of how certain
individuals depend on the effect of stimulants to augment a
hyperactive, restless lifestyle and an exaggerated need for
self-sufficiency. The following case illustrates how stimulants may be used in this way.

A 22-year-old white, single male sought treatment
because of compulsive drug use despite complications
in his physical health and much upheaval in his family
life resulting from his drug dependency. His history
established that he was an individual who had always
been extremely active, restless, and competitive. It
was later learned that athletic prowess, which he insisted he always had, was highly valued in his family.
His father and his two younger siblings, both boys, were

accomplished athletes, and competition among them mani-
fested itself in flagrant challenges and recurrent, thin-
ly disguised contests. The patient also described the
reputation he earned in early adolescence by doing the
wildest, most outlandish, and dangerous things. Before
discovering cocaine, he used marijuana heavily, emphasizing how it helped him to slow down and mellow,
especially if he wished to stay in one place to enjoy
music, an evening of conversation, or a motion picture.
Subsequently he became heavily dependent on cocaine
and stressed, with exhilaration and enthusiasm, how
cocaine complemented his personality and helped him
to remain active, effective, and mobile, particularly
in his athletic, business, and social involvements. He
said, "It was the only drug that relaxed me and gave me
a good feeling." Opiate dependence followed when he
began using increasing amounts of heroin to counteract
the crashing letdown and feelings of inadequacy and
impotence subsequent to cocaine withdrawal.

The foregoing describes the appeal that stimulants hold
for some individuals but says little about problems with
impulsivity associated with these drugs. Stimulants augment
both libidinal and aggressive drives. For individuals who
are depressed and/or those whose self-esteem depends on
maintaining high performance and activity levels, the pre-
sumed relation between these drugs and improved subjective
states and behavior results from the increased mobilization
of energy in aggressive drives. Unfortunately in many
instances, the mobilized aggression exceeds the individual's
capacity to harness and use it adaptively, and it is in
these circumstances that impulse problems are precipitated
by use of stimulants. In some cases problems with aggression
and impulsivity are directly related to mobilized rage and
violent feelings.

A 26-year-old man described how amphetamines originally appealed to him in his late teenage years because they helped him overcome feelings of vulnerability
and weakness in social situations and in contact sports
(despite his hefty muscular physique). With continued
use, however, he found himself repeatedly involved in
brutally damaging fights, both for himself and his
victims. In some instances the fights were provoked
and premeditated, but in other instances they erupted

unpredictably and precipitously with little or no pro-
vocation. Initially he rationalized and glorified these
episodes in a manner consistent with his need to maintain a sense of omnipotence and invulnerability. Later,
upon more sober reflection, he admitted to acute terror
and dysphoria as a result of his uncontrollable impulses while under the influence of stimulants.

Much of the bizarre, explosive, and dangerous behavior
associated with amphetamine use is the result of acting upon
drug-induced psychotic and delusional thinking. At these
times feelings of violence and aggression are projected upon
and subsequently perceived in others and in the surroundings
as hostile and threatening. Paranoid thinking focused on
menacing and terrifying ideas and content is not uncommon
and is often the basis on which individuals attack and retaliate. Unfortunately, as the following case excerpt illustrates, imagined attackers and enemies are often innocent
bystanders.

After almost continuous use of amphetamines over a
two-year period that had increased to very heavy daily
doses, a 24-year-old white male one day began imagining
that passers-by in automobiles suspected that he possessed large amounts of drugs. His preoccupation es-
calated to terror as he descended into the nearby subway station and ran through the tunnel to the next
station in the vicinity of his father's home, for which
he headed. In his mad dash he fantasized a scenario
in which menacing police with messages coming from
their radios were pursuing him. Upon arriving at his
father's home, which was empty at the time, he imagined
that all the windows of the surrounding houses were
focused on him. Losing more and more contact, he sought
out and gathered up his father's guns to protect himself. Upon returning home, the father was almost shot
as this man blasted away with the guns down the corridor
of the house, thinking his father was the police.

From these last two examples it should be abundantly
clear that stimulant drugs can profoundly influence and produce impulsive, dangerous behavior. Over the past ten years
an extensive literature has documented the devastating,
destructive consequences of amphetamine use and dependence
(Griffith, 1966; Lemere, 1966; Kramer, 1969; Ellinwood, 1971;

Shader, 1972; Grinspoon and Hedblom, 1974). I am convinced
that in the majority of instances, amphetamines are used in
an adaptive, relatively benign and/or self-limited way.
However, when used heavily over a prolonged period of time,
they cause extremely violent, dangerous, and impulsive behavior, and represent one of the most dangerous types of
misused drugs.

Sedatives/Hypnotics

Fenichel's observation (1945) that "the super-ego is
that part of the mind that is soluble in alcohol" captures
the basis of appeal for sedatives and hypnotics. Smith and
Wesson (1974) designated this effect of the drugs as "disinhibition euphoria." As previously cited (Khantzian, 1974),
sedatives/hypnotics help to overcome distressful feeling
states associated with anxiety and conflict, which may be
viewed in two ways. These distressing feelings can be seen
as neurotic reactions related to inhibitions and defenses
against unacceptable genital impulses. Or, in my view,
anxiety and conflict leading to heavy dependency on these
drugs are more often associated with personality structures
characterized by rigid and unstable defenses against more
primitive narcissistic longings and aggressive impulses.

Krystal and Raskin (1970) stress the special and exaggerated defenses of denial and splitting employed by
individuals dependent on short-acting sedatives/hypnotics
and alcohol. These defenses are used in the service of
"walling-off" and suppressing aggressive and loving feelings
in relation to the self and others. These authors emphasize
the great difficulty these individuals have with feelings
of ambivalence, and how they prefer to use short-acting drugs
to experience and give vent to such feelings briefly and
therefore "safely."

Although Kohut (1971) and Kernberg (1975) do not specify
particular drug actions, they too refer to the prominence
of massive repression, the splitting mechanism, and other
rigid defenses in addicts. Kohut refers to developmental
trauma and narcissistic disturbances in addicts that result
in failures to internalize caring and protective functions
for the self in the ego. Drugs consequently compensate for
"a defect in the psychological structure." Hypnotics can

overcome rigid and overdrawn defenses and can facilitate and
regulate the expression of affectionate or aggressive feelings in the absence of ego structures that help to modulate
such affects and drives. For these reasons they are welcomed
by individuals with rigid and exaggerated defenses, as well
as those who experience the absence of controls and modula-
tion of impulses. However, the balance between adaptive
release or regulation of feelings and a potentially destructive disinhibition of impulses is a precarious one with these
drugs, often resulting in impulsive and threatening behavior.

A 22-year-old divorcée described both the adaptive and
maladaptive effects of barbiturates for her. She said
she started using barbiturates in her late teens to
adopt an "I-don't-care" attitude after her husband left
her, and that the barbiturates helped her "deal with"
her feelings of sadness and resentment. She preferred
barbiturates to alcohol because she could readily obtain
just the desired subjective effect by limiting herself
to two 100 mgm capsules, whereas she could not regulate
alcohol as well and became "sloppy." More important,
she stressed that barbiturates helped her to overcome
her "up-tightness" so that she could begin to date and
enjoy herself in the company of other men. In contrast
to alcohol, she emphasized that she could "loosen up"
just enough with the barbiturates to overcome her inhibitions about socializing in barrooms and seeking male
companionship. Subsequently she began to experience
increasing irritability and uncontrollable anger in
various relationships when using the drug. The reactions of anger began to escalate with continued and
increasing use, to the point where she felt like actually killing people in the middle of an argument. At
about this same time she became involved with a man who
was a heroin addict and she too became thoroughly addicted. She made sharp contrasts between the effects
of heroin and barbiturates, reporting that heroin helped
her to feel "peaceful and in control" and that she found
companionship to be more easy and comfortable with the
use of heroin.

With this patient, an obvious shift occurred over time
in the way she used and experienced drugs. At the outset,
her troubled feelings and inhibitions caused her repeatedly
to seek out a drug effect to overcome her depression, isola-

tion, and loneliness. However, with protracted use, she found herself increasingly unable to regulate her feelings, and the same drug produced mounting and uncontrollable outbursts of aggression and killer rage. In other cases, however, the use of these drugs is associated with a long-standing history of impulsivity predating drug use and dependency, as exemplified by the following excerpt.

A 23-year-old convicted felon with a history of acute school adjustment problems and delinquent and impulsive behavior going back to his early teen years was admitted to a polydrug treatment unit as part of a prison pre-release rehabilitation program. He was dishonorably discharged from the Army because of charges involving larceny and stolen goods.

His 14-month imprisonment in the maximum security jail from which he had just been released was the result of a drug/alcohol incident. After an evening of moderately heavy drinking with friends and after ingesting several barbiturate capsules, he agreed to accompany one of these friends to the home of another acquaintance whom they abducted with the intention of committing robbery. When their intended victim resisted, the patient reacted by violently and uncontrollably beating and pummelling the man, as well as threatening him with a knife. He and his companion were ultimately apprehended, convicted, and incarcerated.

In reviewing his drug history the patient reported that during his mid-teens, he and his contemporaries did not use drugs but did drink alcohol (mostly beer). He said that he generally avoided drugs, except for five or six instances of combining alcohol with barbiturates, including the instance that resulted in imprisonment. He stated that when he was a teenager, alcohol made him jovial and relaxed, but that this could shift quickly to irritability and angry outbursts. In looking back to his teenage reactions with alcohol and in reviewing the drug/alcohol episode of assault that led to confinement, he indicated that he had discovered in himself terrifying and violent feelings which he "never wanted to come out again." He said he tended to become particularly irritable and violent when someone had done a favor for him for which he believed the other person expected something in return. In the course of the interview he repeatedly resorted to such justification and projections. (The therapist subsequently learned that such reaction was related to long-standing bitterness and resentment toward his mother, who had abandoned him to the care of his maternal grandmother when he was two years old.)

This man apparently realized the potential devastating danger of his impulsivity as a result of shaky impulse controls, especially when under the influence of alcohol or sedative drugs. That he was not entirely without controls was evident in his own deliberate attempts to limit his drug use, his horror and fear of the magnitude and intensity of his rage, and his convincing desire for help and treatment. However, it was equally evident from his past and recent history that he had been only barely, if at all, able to manage his feelings and impulses, with tenuous to nonexistent controls in many instances and rigid denial and projection in others. Similarly, his past delinquent behavior and misconduct suggested a poorly developed ego and means of impulse control, evidenced by the unreflective and insufficiently anxious quality with which he anticipated trouble and danger.

Opiates

More than any other drug, opiates, and heroin in particular, have been associated with violence and crime. This link has been condensed, distorted, and translated into terms such as "crimes of violence," "drug-crazed junkies" and "killer heroin," and reflects public concern and alarm about heroin addicts as impulsive, intimidating people. The criminal behavior associated with heroin addiction is not primarily one of crimes associated with violence or attack on other individuals (Patch et al., 1973a and Patch et al., 1973b). Rather, criminality is associated more with property theft (breaking and entering and robbery) and is the result of stringent arrest laws against opiate possession and the requirement of large amounts of cash to maintain the expensive heroin habit. Rather than producing violent behavior, opiates are, in my opinion, more sought after to produce the opposite effect.

Previous formulations have stressed either the euphoro-
genic-pleasurable effect of narcotics and/or their ability
to relieve a range of distressful or unpleasant affects in
explanation of their powerful tendency to induce and sustain
addiction. Although these formulations have merit, I have
been more impressed with the specific muting and stabilizing
action of narcotics on the individual's rage and aggressive
drives.

After evaluation and treatment of over 200 addicts,
developmental impairments and deficiencies in the egos of
the narcotic addicts seemed paramount (Khantzian, 1974).
These deficiencies were reflected in outbursts of rage, poor
impulse control, and a general sense of dysphoria resulting
from the felt threat to themselves and others because of
their violent feelings and impulses. I was repeatedly impressed with the addicts' subjective reports of their initial experience with opiates in which they discovered the
immediate calming and stabilizing action of the drug. More
specifically, in the course of responding to a carefully taken
drug history, patients gave ample descriptions of dysphoric
states of bodily tensions and restlessness, anger, rage,
violent feelings, and depression that were relieved by heroin
and other opiates. With almost monotonous regularity, patients used terms such as "relaxed," "mellow," and "calming,"
and emphasized a total body response to describe the effects
of opiates when they first began to use such drugs.

On the basis of these findings we hypothesized that individuals were predisposed and became addicted to opiates
because they discovered the stabilizing action of these
drugs on their egos. The short-term effect of the drugs acted
specifically to reverse regressive states by attenuating and
making more bearable painful drives and affects involving
aggression, rage, and related depression. The following case
illustrates some of these effects of opiates on aggressive
and violent behavior.

A 29-year-old white upper-class male heroin addict
sought psychotherapy after starting on an outpatient
methadone maintenance program. At the time of his
evaluation he appeared to be subdued, friendly, and compliant, and related to the therapist in a strikingly
reticent and apologetic manner. In reviewing his past
history he tended to characterize his parents in ideal-

istic terms and stressed his own culpability and guilt
in relation to them and the troubles that had emanated
from his drug use.

His presenting qualities and manner contrasted sharply
with a history of violent, sadistic behavior that dated
back to his teenage years when he was in many provoked
and unprovoked fights. Some of these occurred while
under the influence of sedatives and amphetamines. He
had prided himself on his fearlessness and capacity
for brutality. However, as he approached his early
twenties, he found that his often uncontrollable rage
and violence interfered with his friendships and his
work. It was during this period of his life that he
discovered the calming and subduing influence of heroin,
to which he subsequently became heavily addicted. He
stressed how tranquil and relaxed he felt with heroin,
in contrast to amphetamines and sedatives, and how at
first it helped him to feel organized, more energetic,
and able to work.

During the initial phases of psychotherapy he continued
to present himself in a subdued and deferential way,
speaking politely and thoughtfully about his life, his
parents with whom he remained very involved, and his
estranged wife. This was during a period of stabiliza-
tion with methadone maintenance and at a time when he
was on good terms with his family and was working regularly in his father's business. After approximately
three months of treatment he decided to detoxify from
methadone. As he approached the end of the detoxification a dramatic shift in his manner, attitudes, speech,
and behavior occurred. He was visibly more restless and
uneasy during his interviews, he began to falter at work,
and he became involved in a barroom fight, sustaining a
deep gash in his leg. Repeated fights ensued with his
parents, and he heaped vitriolic hatred and obscenities
on them, revealing for the first time impulses to kill
his father. Obscenities and paranoid feelings of jea-
lousy were also directed toward his wife. Within two
months of discontinuing the methadone he dropped out
of treatment.

This is not an atypical picture of many individuals in
methadone treatment programs. Although heroin addicts de-

scribe the calming and stabilizing effects of heroin, the
muting effect on rage and aggression is not as apparent, and
the short-acting nature of the drug, together with repeated
cycles of withdrawal, tend to produce physical and psychological instability and regressed behavior. Because methadone
is long-acting, addicts are able to use its muting and anti-
aggression action more adaptively, and thereby reverse their
regressed states--an action of the drug accounting for the
dramatic improvement in behavior often seen in methadone-
program participants. Conversely, as Wurmser (1977) has observed and as I have witnessed, there is an almost predict-
able reemergence of impulsive behavior, aggression, and rage
as narcotic addicts withdraw from methadone or other opiates.
Because opiates counteract disorganizing rage, aggression,
and associated dysphoria, we have hypothesized that narcotic
addicts are predisposed to become dependent on opiates. That
is, rather than opiate dependence causing impulsive behavior,
we believe that impulse problems may predispose to and cause
opiate dependence.

Summary and Conclusions

This paper has attempted to review how specific psychopharmacologic effects of distinctive drugs interact with
different personality structures of drug-dependent individuals
to influence behavior. I have stressed drug effects in relation to impulses, particularly aggressive impulses, and have
attempted to clarify how drug use/dependency can be viewed in
some instances as attempts of individuals to solve problems
of impulsivity. Too often the mode of solution causes the
very problems the individuals sought to avoid.

In my opinion, undue emphasis has been placed on pleasure, sociopathy, and absence of adequate superego to account
for drug use. Such emphases detract from a more careful
examination of the ego impairments in this patient population. These patients do not suffer because they lack adequate
superego or conscience. They suffer because developmental
ego impairments have rendered them ill-equipped to manage
their feelings, drives, and behavior in relation to themselves
and others. For most, drug use at the outset represents
attempts to solve problems in day-to-day living. For those
that become drug-dependent, the struggle is more extreme and
desperate and, in my experience, represents attempts to compensate for major ego lacks and impairments.

References

Chein, I., Gerard, D.L., Lee, R.S., Rosenfeld, E. 1964. The
    Road to H. New York: Basic Books.
Ellinwood, E. 1971. Assault and homicide associated with
    amphetamine use. Am. J. Psychiat., 127:1170-1175.
Fenichel, O. 1945. The Psychoanalytic Theory of Neurosis.
    New York: W.W. Norton.
Griffith, J. 1966. A study of illicit amphetamine drug
    traffic in Oklahoma City. Am. J. Psychiat., 123:560-
    569.
Grinspoon, L. and Hedblom, P. 1975. The Speed Culture:
    Amphetamine Use and Abuse in America. Cambridge, Mass.:
    Harvard University Press.
Kernberg, O.F. 1975. Borderline Conditions and Pathological
    Narcissism. New York: J. Aronson, Inc.
Khantzian, E.J. 1974. Opiate addiction: A critique of
    theory and some implications for treatment. Am. J.
    Psychother., 28:59-70.
Khantzian, E.J. 1975. Self-selection and progression in drug
    dependence. Psychiatry Digest, 36:19-22.
Kohut, H. 1971. The Analysis of the Self. New York: Inter-
    national Universities Press.
Kramer, J.C. 1969. Introduction to amphetamine abuse. J.
    Psychedelic Drugs, 2:8-13.
Krystal, H. and Raskin, H. A. 1970. Drug Dependence: As-
    pects of Ego Functions. Detroit: Wayne State University
    Press.
Lemere, F. 1966. The danger of amphetamine dependency. Am.
    J. Psychiat., 123:569-571.
Milkman, H. and Frosch, W.A. 1973. On the preferential abuse
    of heroin and amphetamine. J. Nerv. and Ment. Dis.,
    156:242-248.
Patch, V.D., Fisch, A., Levine, M.E., McKenna, G.J., and
    Raynes, A.E. 1973a. Heroin addicts and violent crime.
    In, Proceedings, Fifth National Conference on Methadone
    Treatment, 386-292.
Patch, V.D., Fisch, A., Levine, M.E., McKenna, G.J., and
    Raynes, A.E. 1973b. Urban versus suburban addict crime.
    In, Proceedings, Fifth National Conference on Metha-
    done Treatment, 393-400.
Rado, S. 1933. The psychoanalysis of pharmacothymia. Psy-
    choanal. Q., 2:1-23.
Schildkraut, J.J. 1965. The catecholamine hypothesis of
    affective disorders: A review of supporting evidence.
    Am. J. Psychiat., 122:509-522.

Shader, R. (Ed.) 1972. Psychiatric Complications of Medi-
    cal Drugs. New York: Raven Press.
Smith, D.E. and Wesson, D.R. 1974. Diagnosis and treatment
    of adverse reactions to sedatives-hypnotics. National
    Institute on Drug Abuse, Washington, D.C.
Weider, H. and Kaplan E. 1969. Drug use in adolescents.
    Psychoanal. Study of the Child, 24:399.
Wurmser, L. 1974. Psychoanalytic considerations of the
    etiology of compulsive drug use. J. Am. Psychoanal.
    Assoc., 22:820-843.
Wurmser, L. 1977. Mr. Pecksniff's horse? (Psychodynamics in
    compulsive drug use). In, Psychodynamic Aspects of
    Opiate Dependence. Research Monograph #12, 36-72.
    National Institute on Drug Abuse, Rockville, Maryland.

FITTING DIFFERENT TREATMENT MODES TO PATTERNS OF DRUG USE

Gerald J. McKenna, M.D.

Instructor in Psychiatry, Harvard Medical School
at The Cambridge Hospital, Cambridge, Massachusetts

Professionals dealing with individuals who manifest
problems of addiction, alcoholism, criminal behavior, and
impulsive behavior have, in general, attempted to seek de-
nominators common to all of these problems. This approach
often leads to the creation of a mental set that can severely limit further exploration and critical thinking by therapists or counselors. Whether we care to admit it or not,
terms such as "addict," "alcoholic," or "criminal" arouse
mental images that have been reinforced over time by several
factors: social attitudes toward deviant behavior, media
presentation of individuals or groups manifesting impulsive
behavior, and personal contact or experience of both professionals and lay persons with these individuals. By recognizing that we hold these stereotypic images and attitudes,
at least at some level, we can progress beyond our own pre-
judice and engage in more objective, discriminate thinking
about the relevant factors in assessing the behavior patterns of a particular individual.

This discussion will emphasize the need for individual
diagnostic appraisal and formulation of problems so that any
treatment approach proceeds from the evaluation of a particular individual rather than from a monolithic etiological
conceptualization. Rather than abandoning classification
systems entirely, the approach outlined here will attempt
to examine more closely discrete diagnostic categories for
evidence of diverse etiology in order to determine appropriate treatment for each individual from among diverse treatment approaches.

Theoretical and Therapeutic Limitations

The various professionals involved with individuals manifesting impulsive behavior--psychiatrists, members of the criminal justice system, law enforcement officers, educators, and psychologists--bring to their work divergent education, experience, and conceptual tools. We do not share a common theoretical understanding of the origins of the problems we are attempting to address. Nor do we have a consistent theoretical framework for understanding addiction, impulsiveness, delinquency, and criminal behavior. The joint endeavor of all who work in this field is to explore in greater depth the variety of theoretical concepts and clinical approaches to individuals with these disorders.

Psychiatry, as an institution and a branch of medicine, has not paid particular attention to problems of addiction, delinquency, criminality, and impulsive behavior. Texts on psychiatry reflect this inattention. They usually include all these problems under the broad term "character disorders," which carries both a negative connotation and the implication of untreatability. The implication that certain individuals or groups are untreatable is both an observation and a criticism--an observation because it reflects what most psychiatrists are taught in fairly traditional psychiatric training programs; and a criticism because it reflects a faulty a priori judgment. It is more accurate to say that the therapeutic techniques taught in psychiatric training programs are inadequate for treating some individuals than to say that some individuals are untreatable. The latter position merely dismisses the problem; the former implies a need to formulate new theoretical frameworks and develop new therapeutic techniques.

In looking at patterns of drug use as one example of impulsive behavior, it soon becomes apparent that etiology of the drug use, types of drugs used, and degree of involvement are all important factors in determining appropriate interventions. While it is not within the scope of this discussion to review in detail all of the patterns and etiologies of drug use, some important and recurrent patterns will be reviewed to illustrate the need for careful individual diagnostic evaluation.

Drug Use as Self-Treatment for Psychological Distress

Much of the discussion that follows is the result of my experience in working with drug-dependent individuals in a variety of settings, both inpatient and outpatient, military and civilian, in prisons and in an outpatient court clinic. In both narcotics and polydrug treatment programs with which I have been actively involved, we have realized that a considerable number of patients who are either narcotics dependent or multiple-drug dependent use drugs as self-treatment for symptoms of psychological distress. This psychological distress can range across the entire spectrum of psychiatric syndromes. Since most of those who came to these programs showed a severe degree of drug involvement, we tended to see more severe degrees of psychopathology accompanying the drug use. One hypothesis, though not supported by data in our work, is that lesser degrees of drug involvement would coincide with lesser degrees of psychopathology. We administered the Psychiatric Status Schedule of Spitzer and Endicott to over 150 individuals in our inpatient detoxification/treatment program with narcotic, alcohol, and/or multiple-substance-dependency problems. The overall finding for all groups (McKenna, 1977; McKenna & Khantzian, 1977) is that a very high degree of psychopathology exists in the population that sought treatment at this facility. Similar findings by others suggest that a high degree of psychopathology may be common to all polydrug or multiple-substance-dependent individuals (Benvenuto & Bourne, 1975).

What is important in evaluating a drug-dependent individual is to recognize the existence of psychopathology, to specify its nature, and to institute appropriate treatment. Among the more severe psychiatric syndromes we have encountered are psychotic states, severe depression, and borderline states. Less severe patterns of drug use have been associated with various neurotic patterns involving phobias and anxiety states. A variety of psychophysiological problems have also been noted, particularly chronic pain states as manifestations of character patterns. Some individuals with chronic pain states show low tolerance to pain, heavy drug use to "treat" the pain, and a tendency to form highly dependent relationships on family members and therapists.

Psychotic States

In a paper presented a few years ago (McKenna, et al.,
1973), the use of narcotics as self-treatment for psychosis
was discussed. Case histories were presented in which three
individuals with a variety of psychotic states (including
manic-depressive psychosis, psychotic depression, and schizophrenia) attempted to treat these conditions through the
use of narcotics. While this "treatment" was successful to
varying degrees, it nonetheless became clear that narcotics
act as powerful psychotropic agents, able in at least some
instances to control or modify psychotic symptoms. These
individuals were on methadone maintenance, and methadone
served the same antipsychotic function. During or shortly
after completion of detoxification from methadone, psychotic
symptoms recurred. (Patients also reported onset of psychotic symptoms after previous attempts to detoxify from
heroin.) In the case of the individual with manic-depressive psychosis (whose manic and, later, depressive symptoms
recurred in each of three detoxifications over a several-
year period), symptoms of his illness were controlled through
treatment with lithium carbonate and psychotherapy. This
patient was able to refrain from narcotics use as long as he
remained on lithium; his main reason for using narcotics--
to control psychotic symptoms--was no longer present. Similarly, another individual who developed schizophrenic symptoms (auditory hallucinations, paranoid delusions, and other
evidence of major thought disorder) was able, upon detoxification, to obtain symptomatic relief when treated with
phenothiazines.

In the hospital narcotics treatment program with which
I am presently associated, we have found, upon careful clinical investigation and thorough review of patient histories,
that approximately 10 percent of our patients have histories
similar to those of individuals with diagnosis of a major
psychosis. This same percentage of similar histories was
noted among individuals participating in another methadone
maintenance program (some of whom were described above).
This does not imply that 10 percent of narcotics addicts
suffer a psychotic illness but, rather, that among individuals
seeking treatment for narcotics addiction in methadone maintenance programs, a history of psychosis can be expected in
a percentage that is greater than that for the population as
a whole.

The treatment implications for narcotics addicts with psychotic illness are profound and complicated. It is often not sufficient to substitute an antipsychotic agent for the narcotic and then perhaps refer the patient to a traditional psychiatric clinic. First of all, these individuals often have been addicted for years and have identities inexorably tied to the narcotics subculture. In addition, some would prefer to think of themselves as narcotics addicts than as psychiatric patients. A treatment program must take these factors into account and formulate treatment plans accordingly. In instances where an individual continues to be treated in a drug treatment program, staff must keep in mind that detoxification from the narcotic (or other drugs) may necessitate the institution of appropriate antipsychotic medication.

Depressive States

Among many patients in drug-treatment programs, we are beginning to recognize depression as a significant clinical entity. Whether the depression is primary (preceding the addiction and etiologically related to it) or secondary (occurring subsequent to and precipitated by the addiction) is not clear, but the depressive syndrome with classical signs is present in patients under treatment for narcotics addiction. It interferes with patterns of living, the process of treatment, and may contribute to continued drug use for relief of symptoms.

A growing literature documents depression among narcotics addicts, especially those on methadone maintenance. In a recent study, Weissman, et al. (1976) found an incidence of moderate depression in approximately one third of 106 patients in a methadone maintenance clinic in New Haven using standard tests for depression (Raskin Depression Scale, Hamilton Rating Scale for Depression, Hopkins Symptom Checklist). These results were consistent with those found by Senay (1977) in Chicago. One pilot study by Woody, et al. (1975) in Philadelphia treated depression in narcotics addicts with doxepin HCl in a double-blind study. Their preliminary results indicate that the use of tricyclics is a useful adjunct in the treatment of depressed narcotics addicts; it results in less drug use outside the clinic, a longer period of time spent in counseling, and reports of subjective symptomatic improvement by both staff and patients. Reduction of depressive symptoms was also demonstrated by significant changes on standard scales for depression.

The telling point here is that it is necessary to look beyond the presenting complaints of a narcotics user for symptoms of a psychiatric disorder which might be ameliorated by the judicious use of psychotropic medication—in this case the antidepressants—accompanied by a program of individual and/or group psychotherapy. This is a difficult concept for many in the field of addiction to accept since there has been such a traditional reluctance to use psychotropic agents in a population that tends to misuse other psychotropic agents (and indeed all drugs that are misused are psychotropic or they would not be used at all). Misuse, however, occurs when addicts attempt to self-treat their symptoms by using drugs in an uncontrolled manner. With proper diagnosis and monitoring by medical personnel, psychotropic drugs (preferably nonaddicting ones) can be used in treating the underlying psychiatric condition; if symptomatic relief results, the addictive cycle may be broken. This may also facilitate establishing meaningful therapeutic relationships between the drug-dependent clients and their counselors.

Adolescent Drug Use

In the late 1960s and early 1970s, public panic emerged concerning the burgeoning use of drugs by adolescents. The assumption (which was to a large extent correct) was that this behavior pattern in adolescents was part of a broader rejection of establishment values and a rebellion against established authority. Although the means to the end were different, this pattern of adolescent experimentation with "the dangerous" and the rejection of adult authority was in fact not qualitatively different than it had been in past eras. The great fear was that experimentation with drugs would lead to a generation of addicts. This fear was unfounded, and we came to realize that most adolescent drug use was part of the process of experimentation which is the hallmark of adolescence. Therefore, for most adolescents found with a reefer in their pockets, no therapeutic intervention was or is necessary. It is probable, though, that a small percentage of adolescents who experiment with drugs could become psychologically and/or physically dependent on

addictive substances. This percentage probably remains constant for each generation and culture and reflects the attitudes of the culture as a whole toward substance use and
abuse, as well as individual susceptibility to substance
dependence.

When confronted with an adolescent who uses drugs, the
assumption should not be made that a serious problem exists
until a thorough understanding of the type of drug, reasons
for use, and degree of involvement have been evaluated. This
process should, in fact, be applied whenever one is evaluating
any drug use pattern.

Situational Drug Use and Addiction

The instance of situational drug use and addiction is
mentioned here to put in some perspective our notions about
drug use in general and the dangers of so-called hard drug
use in particular. Experience has shown that significant
numbers of individuals can use highly addicting drugs for
extended periods under situations of stress without becoming
life-long addicts. This concept was borne out during the war
in Southeast Asia when thousands of American soldiers became physically addicted to powerful drugs (including heroin,
barbiturates, and alcohol) or engaged in daily use of nonaddicting but equally powerful drugs such as high-grade marijuana. Most of these soldiers viewed their drug use as
situational and time-limited. The drugs helped them cope
with the physical and psychological pressures of a war that
was unpopular and of life in a strange and hostile place
where no one could be trusted and the enemy was everywhere
(McKenna & Mirin, 1973; Mirin & McKenna, 1975). Each man
knew that he had only to survive for 365 days and his particular trip into Armageddon would be over. The thought of
thousands of addicted soldiers returning to the United
States caused serious concern in the nation. It was quickly discovered, however, that most of the addicted men were
able to discontinue their habits (especially heroin) prior
to returning to the United States. Even among those who
could not discontinue heroin use prior to returning and were
"caught" in the mandatory urinalysis screening program,
relatively few continued a pattern of heroin addiction once
back in the States (Robins, 1973).

The case of situational drug use points out that not
every case of addiction, even to drugs such as heroin, needs
vigorous and prolonged intervention. As has been emphasized
previously, careful history should elucidate the causes of
drug use, and in the case of situational drug use (whatever
drug is involved), relatively short-term therapy may be sufficient.

Drug Use to Augment Character Style

This type of drug use may, in fact, be operative in the
greatest percentage of drug dependent individuals who seek
treatment, although this statement cannot currently be sub-
stantiated. Character traits or styles frequently found in
this group include the sociopathic, the narcissistic, and
the antisocial. When successful, persons with these traits
are rarely found in prisons or drug treatment programs; when
unsuccessful, they frequently turn to drug use to manage the
frustration that accompanies their unattained goals and as-
suages their "entitled" view of themselves. Often they form
the core of the prison population.

Treatment of this particular group is most difficult
since traditional counseling methods have little or no relevance. With sufficient time in a prison setting, some progress may be made, but traditional treatment in an outpatient setting has little chance of success. Special forms of
treatment that initially focus solely on cognitive processes
have a better chance of success since they deal with those
intellectual aspects of the individual which are concrete
and most familiar. A system of educational counseling such
as "Thresholds," developed by Burglass and Duffy (1974),
should be initiated. This counseling approach is cognitively
oriented, curricular in format, and focuses on the decision-
making process. Its main purpose is to demonstrate that
individuals have a number of choices in any given situation,
and that they can choose options most beneficial to them and
take sole responsibility for those decisions. Later in the
course of treatment, it may be appropriate to address other
issues in the individual's life. When this course is pur-
sued, a more direct, confrontation approach--which continually
challenges the individual's manner of interacting, patterns
of behavior, and ultimately, patterns of defense--has been
found more useful than a passive, nondirect approach. In-

dividuals who can sustain this treatment mode when motivated
(regardless of the reasons for the motivation) often fare
well in residential treatment programs that emphasize confrontation and are staffed by ex-addicts or ex-offenders.
The individual quickly learns that he cannot "con" in such
a setting, and the usual character defenses of projection,
denial, and entitlement are gradually abandoned. The use of
medication in this group is to be discouraged.

The Need for Flexibility in the Therapist

Drug-dependent individuals manifest a variety of clinical pictures demanding careful diagnostic appraisal and
individualization of treatment plan. Though this discussion
focuses on the drug-dependent individual as representing
only one type of impulsive person, the same careful evaluation should occur with persons manifesting other types of
problems involving impulsive behavior. This puts a special
demand for flexibility on the therapist or counselor who
must, especially with impulsive clients, adjust his inter-
active style to meet the needs of the individual. (Curious-
ly, this flexibility is often not taught to drug treatment
counselors and others treating impulsive clients). In the
case of highly impulsive character problems, this will involve
an active engagement of the individual, attention to interaction patterns, and setting reasonable limits. The action
defenses employed by such individuals and the frequent use
of projection serve to keep them emotionally distant from
others. Unless these defenses are interrupted, there is
little chance for forming a relationship with a therapist.
As mentioned earlier, it can be useful to approach such
individuals on a cognitive level, since dealing with cognitive processes is generally less threatening than dealing
with affective issues.

When treating more emotionally disorganized individuals
(such as many multiple-substance or polydrug abusers), a
more supportive approach is indicated. Early findings of the
National Polydrug Study (Benvenuto & Bourne, 1975) showed
that many residential treatment programs using a highly
confrontational approach were uniformly unsuccessful in
treating polydrug users with significant overt psychopathology. These individuals tended to benefit more from a traditional psychiatric inpatient environment.

The use of psychotropic medication is indicated in the treatment of some individuals with impulse problems whether related to use of drugs, alcohol, or involvement in criminal behavior. Again, it is only through the counselor's sophistication and sensitivity to the presence of a condition ameliorable by use of medication that such a determination can be made. An evaluation by a physician is necessary for the prescription of any medication, but unless physician or psychiatrist evaluations are routine in a given program, the initial determination of the probability of a coexisting depression or even psychotic disorder must be made by the counselor.

This need for therapist flexibility necessitates a fairly comprehensive training program for counselors and the need for continuing education. In training programs where this need has been addressed, one result, I believe, is that the counselors (who are primarily mental health workers and nurses) are becoming more aware of the variety of causes of impulsive behavior and are able to tailor the treatment plans to the needs of each individual.

Summary

Impulsive behavior is seen in a variety of human conditions that include delinquency, criminality, drug dependence, and alcoholism. The causes of each of these conditions are complex, and at present there is no uniform theory that explains each one. Unfortunately, however, popular myths have arisen surrounding each condition which have little if any foundation in fact. The primary danger in accepting these myths is that they limit our discriminate thinking about each of these problems and, consequently, their solutions.

The various patterns of drug use illustrate the nature and complexity of drug dependence as a human condition. As the etiology of the drug dependence varies, so the treatment approach should vary to meet the particular needs of the individual.

References

Benvenuto, J. and Bourne, P.G. 1975. The Federal polydrug abuse project: Initial report. J. Psychedelic Drugs, Vol. 7, No. 2.

Burglass, M. and Duffy, M.G. 1974. Thresholds Teacher's Manual. Cambridge, Mass.: Correctional Solutions Foundation, Inc.

McKenna, G.J. 1977. The drug/alcohol/psychiatry interface. Proceedings of the Third National Drug Abuse Conference. New York: Marcel-Dekker, Inc.

McKenna, G.J., Fisch, A., Levine, M., Patch, V., and Raynes, A. 1973. The use of methadone as a psychotropic agent. Proceedings of the Fifth National Methadone Conference, Washington, D.C.

McKenna, G.J. and Khantzian, E.J. Diagnosis and management of acute drug problems. Internatl. J. of Addictions (in press).

McKenna, G.J. and Mirin, S. 1973. Drug use in Southeast Asia: A situational response. Presented at the American Psychiatric Association Annual Meeting, Honolulu, Hawaii.

Mirin, S. and McKenna, G.J. 1975. Adjustment in the combat zone: The role of marijuana use. Military Medicine, Vol. 104.

Robins, L.N. 1973. The Vietnam drug user returns. Special Action Office Monograph, Series A., No. 2, Washington, D.C.: U.S. Govt. Printing Office.

Senay, E. 1976. Personal communication.

Weissman, M.M., Slobetz, F., Prusoff, B., Mezritz, M., and Howard, P. 1976. Clinical depression among narcotics addicts maintained on methadone in the community. Am. J. Psychiat., 133, 1434-1438.

Woody, G.E., O'Brien, C.P., and Rickels, K. 1975. Depression and anxiety in heroin addicts: A placebo-controlled study of doxepin in combination with methadone. Am. J. Psychiat., 132, 447-450.

Part III

The Impulsive Patient and the Criminal Justice System

LAW, MENTAL HEALTH, AND IMPULSIVE PATIENTS

David Reisen, M.D.

Instructor in Psychiatry, Harvard Medical School
at The Cambridge Hospital, Cambridge, Massachusetts

In recent years a number of factors have coalesced to
intensify the interaction of law and mental health, and much
of this activity has revealed the complexity of several important issues facing both the legal and the psychiatric professions. Salient reasons promoting this interaction emerge
from some current social trends and their concomitant facts:
increasing numbers of persons have used and will continue
to come into contact with the institutional contexts in which
the two disciplines interact; law schools are attracting more
persons interested in mental health and prison systems reform; and government support of reform in these areas will
necessarily heighten interdisciplinary activity.

Critical Issues

Several key issues at the interface of both disciplines
are of particular interest to professionals dealing with patients with impulse disorders: the right to treatment, the
right to refuse treatment, the nature of informed consent,
and the questions raised by the Tarasoff (1974) decision in
California. In general, the psychiatric literature has
lacked thoughtful discussions of the legal aspects of these
issues (Cleary, 1973; Liss and Frances, 1975), and the legal
literature, in like manner, has not explored their implications sufficiently (Brakel and Rock, 1971; Zwerdling, 1975).

The issues just mentioned apply especially to impulsive
persons because in general the judicial system is mobilized

to action by the behavior of this population. Although much
of the recent discussion of law, psychiatry, and the impulsive person has been on a theoretical level, it must be emphasized that our current institutions for the treatment of
these people continue to be woefully understaffed with professionals and still resemble the warehouses they are so often
accused of being in lawsuits. Many of these suits are good
faith attempts to remedy execrable conditions. As the staffs
of these institutions struggle to cope with often violent
patients, recourse to the forceable use of medications,
restraints, and seclusions becomes inevitable. The impulsiveness of patients which calls forth these responses also brings
in its wake the equally inevitable legal proceedings aimed at
correcting abuses.

     In this paper I will discuss the four areas mentioned
above that have commanded the most attention in recent years.
I shall then cite individual cases and briefly analyze their
psychodynamics in order to present the law and mental health
interface as it may affect particular patients from the therapist's perspective.

     Because conflicting decisions among different jurisdic-
tions abound in case and statutory law, definitive determina-
tions on many issues are nonexistent. However, despite the
complexity of these issues and the statutory contradictions
that prevail, mental health professionals can benefit from
awareness of developing legal trends in areas that will continue to affect patients and treatment.

The Right to Treatment

     First discussed by Birnbaum (1960) in an article in the
American Bar Association Journal, the right-to-treatment concept lay moot in case law until the District of Columbia Court
of Appeals decided, in Rouse v. Cameron (1966), that a person committed involuntarily had a right in law to be treated.
The facts of the case were: Clarence Rouse had been found
not guilty by reason of insanity on a charge of carrying a
deadly weapon, a misdemeanor punishable by a maximum of a
year's imprisonment. After spending three years in a public
mental hospital, where he had been sent for treatment, Rouse's
lawyer asked the court, through a writ of habeas corpus,
for his release because he was allegedly receiving no treat-

ment. Judge Bazelon noted that the purpose of involuntary
confinement is treatment, not punishment, and that hospitalization without treatment calls into question the constitu-
tionality of the confinement (Slovenko, 1973).

Similar decisions followed in several state courts
(Patuxent v. Daniels, 1966), but the most expansive thus far
occurred in Wyatt v. Stickney (1971, 1972), a case concerning an Alabama state hospital. There the court found that
a constitutional right to treatment did exist and ordered
the institution to meet certain minimum standards of staffing, physical care of patients, and so forth.

This decision provided the impetus to guarantee involuntarily committed mental patients the right to receive
treatment. What the law has not broached, as yet, is a
definition of "treatment." At what institutional and financial level can treatment take place? Is individual psychotherapy required? How frequently must one's treatment plan
be reevaluated to qualify what is being offered as treatment
rather than mere custodial care? Thus far the courts have
not set standards for treatment in order to avoid infringe-
ment on the health professions' domain. Mental health workers should attempt to use this as an opportunity to be in the
vanguard for improvement of services--not only for impulsive
patients but for all citizens--within a framework consonant
with the preservation of civil rights.

Along with the right to treatment issue, the issue of
feasible treatment arises. What constraints are there on
what we can offer clients?

Because therapies for persons with impulse disorders
have not been notably successful in the past, there has been
a great impetus to seize upon newer developments and apply
them to this population. For example, psychosurgery was once
looked to by some as a panacea for controlling chronically
violent patients, while aversive conditioning has been tried
more recently by others in an effort to reform prisoners.
The case law in these areas is skimpy and legislative acts
even rarer, but it appears that the "hands off" doctrine
in law has applied here also. There is, to my knowledge, no
jurisdiction that flatly bans psychosurgery or aversive conditioning. The approach of the law has been to view these
matters on a case-by-case basis, and clear guidelines do not
exist.

A final aspect of the right to treatment issue is the
consequence of nontreatment. For voluntary patients this is
not an issue, but as the recent O'Connor v. Donaldson (1974)
decision shows, there may be profound sequellae to mental
health professionals for not offering therapy to the involuntarily committed, especially if they are not dangerous.
Hailed by reformers as a major step forward for patients'
rights, the Donaldson decision was drawn narrowly. The Court
held that "when a patient is not dangerous to himself or
others and, if he is mentally ill, is not currently receiving
any treatment, he must be released from custody at his own
request" (Curran 1975). The Court did not deal with the
difficult question posed by mentally ill, impulsive persons
who are dangerous: Can they be held involuntarily without
treatment in hospitals? The ultimate outcome of this issue
still is in doubt.

In the final outcome of O'Connor v. Donaldson, the defendant was ordered released and the case was returned to a
lower court for the assessment of damages. These were awarded
in the amount of $38,500 for compensation damages and $10,000
for punitive damages. What should be noted, however, is that
one is not liable, according to this precedent, for damages
unless one knows, or reasonably ought to know, that continuing to confine a nonviolent person against his desire and
without treatment violates that person's constitutional
rights; or if one takes such action maliciously intending to
deprive the patient of his constitutional rights or to otherwise injure him (Curran, 1975). Clearly if one is providing
reasonable treatment, one avoids liability. However, psychiatrists and courts often differ regarding definitions of
"reasonable treatment."

The Right to Refuse Treatment

Here, also, the case law is conflicting, but the trend
seems clear. The highest values for many involved with these
matters are those of personal liberty and choice; related to
these are values of privacy and the freedom from invasion of
one's body and thoughts. As Justice Brandeis said, dissent-
ing in Olmstead v. United States (1928):

Experience should teach us to be most on our guard to
protect liberty when the Government's purposes are bene-

ficent. Men born to freedom are naturally alert to
repel invasion of their liberty by evil minded rulers.
The greatest dangers to liberty lurk in insidious encroachment by men of zeal, well meaning, but without
understanding.

However, because physicians and other healers have a commitment to health, they feel that the exercise of all liberties is severely compromised when one is ill, physically or
mentally. From this conviction arises the impetus to provide
treatment to repair disordered faculties and thereby permit
the patient to enjoy his rights fully. The problem of me-
diating between different and valued beliefs by professionals
in the two disciplines has led to the issue of the right to
refuse treatment.

Legal justifications for the right to refuse treatment
stem from several sources. The first is the judicial presumption of competency. Although one may be in a prison or
involuntarily committed to a mental hospital, one is held
legally competent unless judicial proceedings have decided
otherwise. Contained in the concept of competency is the
presumption that an individual can decide to accept or refuse
medical treatment. The Supreme Court declared in 1891
(Union Pacific v. Botsford):

> No right is held more sacred, or is more carefully
> guarded, by the common law, than the right of every in-
> dividual to the possession and control of his own person,
> free from all restraint or interference of others, un-
> less by clear and unquestionable authority of law. As
> well said by Justice Cooley, "The right to one's person
> may be said to be a right of complete immunity: to be
> left alone."

If mental health practicioners feel that treatment is
clearly indicated and that a patient is refusing this because he is incapable of making a reasonable decision, a
judicial determination should be sought regarding competency.
If the person is judged incompetent, an independent guardian
can be appointed. If this procedure is not followed and
treatment is forced upon a person who is not clearly in emergency circumstances, the practitioner places himself in a
legally actionable situation.

Another source for the right to refuse treatment is the
fact of its incorporation into law. For example, the Massachusetts Mental Health Law (1971) clearly states that a patient may refuse permission for psychosurgery and electro-
convulsive therapy. A recent California statute (1974)
covers essentially the same areas.

Finally, much case law has frequently demonstrated the
Supreme Court's intention to protect individual liberties
against any attempt at encroachment by the state. For example, the free speech protections of the First Amendment have
been extended to include freedom of thought. In Stanley v.
Georgia (1969), the Court stated, "Our whole constitutional
heritage rebels at the thought of giving government the power
to control men's minds." Another First Amendment right, that
of the freedom of religion, was the basis for the action of
the Second Circuit Court enjoining the state from forcing a
patient to take medicine. In the case at issue (Winters,
1971), the state had forced medication upon a Christian Sci-
entist against her religious beliefs. In exploring these
issues further, Dr. Jay Katz (1969) wrote:

> Questions like the following, about the relationship
> between rights and duties, must soon arise: Does the
> right [to treatment] impose only a correlative duty on
> the state and mental health professionals to provide
> treatment for those persons who wish to exercise such a
> right? Or does this right also impose a duty on the
> person to submit to treatment? If the former, what are
> the consequences for those who do not wish to invoke such
> a right or are unlikely to benefit from treatment? If
> the latter, what kinds of treatment can and should be
> authorized for those who do not wish to be treated, and,
> again, what are the consequences for those who are un-
> likely to benefit from treatment? Rights may impose
> corresponding duties on the individual, but distinc-
> tions should be made between rights which a person can
> waive and those he cannot waive.

A special circumstance arises when a person involuntarily
incarcerated--prisoner or patient--is so acutely ill that
emergency measures are called for. In this case the physician can reasonably act to restrain behavior which might
imminently threaten the life or physical safety of the patient or others. The justification lies in his being an

agent of the state, and he is essentially representing its
police and parens patriae powers. However, the doctrine of
"least restrictive alternative" applies here (Lake v. Cameron,
1966; Covington v. Harris, 1969). This doctrine empowers mental health personnel to intervene, but simultaneously requires that patients' rights are compromised as little as
possible. It is most important that any interventions of an
emergency nature be carefully documented in the patient's
record, for as the District of Columbia court stated in the
Williams (1970) case:

> On their face, the records must be adequate to demon-
> strate the propriety . . . of the challenged decision.
> If the records are not adequate on their face, they may
> not be rehabilitated by a subsequent demonstration in
> court.

In sum, the intent of the law is clear: patients do have
the right to refuse treatment, except in circumstances where
there is a "clear and present danger," and in these rare instances interventions must be minimal and clearly documented.

Quite clearly the right to refuse treatment poses a
practical difficulty. What is to be done with impulsive people who are remanded for care and who refuse what is offered?
The courts have not yet come squarely to grips with this issue, but a reasonable procedure would be to inform the appropriate judicial authority of the situation, advise it of
what one feels to be the available options, and ask for guidance in the matter.

Informed Consent

Although the issues of informed consent and the right
to refuse treatment overlap, recent developments in both the
mental health professions and case law require that the former
be given special attention. The issue was confronted most
directly in the case of Kaimowitz v. Department of Mental
Health (1973). Briefly, the case concerned a psychosurgery
research project, and a major focus of the court's opinion
was on the capacity of the patient to give informed consent.
The court considered three factors as crucial to informed
consent: competency, knowledge of risks, and voluntariness.
Since the procedure was so experimental that the risks were

deemed unknowable, the court voided consent on those grounds.
It also voided consent on the grounds that <u>an involuntary</u>
<u>patient faces subtle but powerful coercive pressures to com-</u>
<u>ply with medical recommendations</u>. To the extent that this is
operative, consent is not voluntary and therefore void.

Taken to an extreme, this argument could vitiate all
consents gained from chronically institutionalized persons,
whether prisoners or patients. However, we need not examine
this extreme. It is enough to realize that more and more we
are being asked to gain carefully informed consent for our
treatments, to document this, and to be certain that the consent was truly informed and freely given. A consultation with
a lawyer attached to the treatment facility or the state department of mental health might be in order to elucidate any
difficulties that might arise in this area.

The Tarasoff Case and the Duty to Warn

One of the major problems confronting therapists who
deal with impulsive people is to balance one's commitment to
individuals in treatment against one's concern for the society
at large. Until quite recently psychotherapy primarily served
the middle and upper classes, and the therapeutic relationship was a voluntary one. Patients with severe impulse disorders rarely saw therapists. As mental health services have
reached more and more people, more knowledge has been gained
by citizens concerning the patient-therapist relationship;
it is no longer totally closeted in the privacy of the consulting room. With this entry into the public spotlight,
problems not previously encountered have arisen. One such
group of issues was posed by the recent <u>Tarasoff</u> case.

In 1969, when Prosenjit Poddar was a student at Berke-
ley, he began dating his roommate's sister, Tatiana Tarasoff,
and also began psychotherapy at the Cowell Memorial Hospital
of the University of California. During his therapy, Poddar expressed his desire to kill his girlfriend to his therapist, a clinical psychologist.

Following this disclosure the therapist consulted with
two psychiatrists and the three decided that Poddar was dangerous to himself and to society and should be involuntarily
committed for observation and treatment. The campus police,

acting on the therapist's written request, interviewed Poddar and chose to take no further action. Upon hearing of the incident, the chief of the department of psychiatry at the hospital ordered that no further action be taken against Poddar. All records concerning the therapist's correspondence with Poddar were ordered destroyed, as well as a substantial portion of the notes concerning the therapy. Neither Miss Tarasoff nor any member of her family was notified of any of these facts, and two months later Poddar shot and stabbed his former girlfriend to death.

An action for wrongful death was brought against the Regents of the University of California (who employed the defendant psychiatrists) by Miss Tarasoff's parents, who alleged, among other things, that the defendants were negligent in failing to warn the victim of the threat of the patient. Although the legal intricacies underlying the decision in this case are beyond the scope of this paper, the clear message of the California Supreme Court (1974) was:

> When a doctor or a psychotherapist, in the exercise of his professional skill and knowledge, determines, or should determine, that a warning is essential to avert danger arising from the medical or psychological condition of his patient, he incurs a legal obligation to give that warning.

Further, the Court held that:

> The public policy favoring protection of the confidential character of patient-psychotherapist communications must yield in instances in which disclosure is essential to avert dangers to others. The protective privilege ends where the public peril begins.

Tarasoff has generated a deluge of publications concerning its wisdom, ignorance, usefulness, and unenforceability (Ayres and Holbrook, 1975; Burns, 1975; Glassman, 1975; Kaplan, 1975; Mirakian, 1976; Valentine, 1975). The major point for mental health workers treating impulsive people, however, is that they may be held liable for damages to a third party, despite their having no formal relationship to that third party.

This situation poses an obvious and difficult problem for a therapist: he must weigh the effect, on the therapeutic

process, of giving warning, against the danger to the threatened party if warning is not given. And he must strive to
strike the proper balance. My own approach is to ask myself
the question, "Why am I being told of this threat now?"
After examining my internal feelings, I would ask the patient
to share with me his or her thoughts about this. My goals
in this inquiry would be several: to assess the patient's
capacities to observe the seriousness of the threat, to contain his or her impulses, and to ally with me in investigating rather than acting. If such a diagnostic investigation
left me still doubting either the patient's ability to restrain
his impulses or my assessment of the situation, I would con-
sult with another professional. Because impulsive persons can
frequently arouse anxiety in a therapist that may diminish
objectivity, another colleague's views are sometimes a prudent
or necessary measure. If doubt still existed after the consultation, or if I had resolved that the person was, in fact,
dangerous, I would move for civil commitment.

Although much data exist to suggest that we overpredict dangerousness (Diamond, 1975; Dershowitz, 1970), when
faced with such problematic situations, one can only depend
upon one's best clinical judgment. Only if all attempts at
commitment failed would I choose to warn. Such a procedure
would then be open to legal question.

Certain commentators on Tarasoff feel that it will undermine the privacy of the patient-therapist relationship
and thereby drive away from therapy just those impulse-
ridden people who would be better off in treatment than not.
Others feel that the decision, if widely implemented, will
reassure those who fear their inability to control their behavior, and that it will encourage therapists to treat more
difficult patients since it gives them license to warn and
thereby unburden themselves.

No one knows what the effect, if any, of this decision
will be. It may lead to a sort of defensive psychotherapy
in which therapists either urge their patients to disclose
nothing threatening or, in contrast, receive all information
and warn excessively. In both instances treatment would be
impeded in the name of avoiding liability. The decision may,
however, stimulate studies concerned with predicting and
controlling dangerousness--a sorely needed research area. In
any event, Tarasoff reveals that mental health professionals

and impulsive patients no longer have a relationship that
lies outside the purview of the judicial system in matters
that may endanger a third party.

Clinical Aspects of Law and Mental Health

Although mental health personnel must be aware of the
status of the laws governing the treatment of impulsive persons, it is my contention that practitioners are brought most
immediately into contact with the judicial system on a clinical level, and the symbolic importance of the legal appara-
tus must not be overlooked. Not only do patients employ the
remedies the law offers when there are wrongs to be righted,
but frequently the judicial mechanism becomes a way for them
to live out intrapsychic conflicts. The two cases and discussion that follow attempt to illustrate this interaction.

Case #1

Mr. DeB., a thirty-three-year-old male, was found not
guilty by reason of insanity on several major but
nonviolent criminal charges in the late 1960s. As a
consequence of a subsequent hearing, he was ordered to
a public psychiatric hospital for treatment. He had previously been at this hospital under different circumstances. Just prior to his arrest and pretrial court-
ordered mental examination at the hospital, he had been
a valued nurse's assistant there. His hiring had come
about in a most unusual manner.

About one year prior to being hired, Mr. DeB. had been
hitchhiking and had gotten a ride from a man who
subsequently invited him to his apartment for a drink.
The driver made a homosexual advance to Mr. DeB., and
Mr. DeB. shot him five times. As the victim was unwilling to testify in court for fear that his homosexuality
would be made public, the prosecution was based on the
charge of the illegal possession of a deadly weapon, and
Mr. DeB. was put on probation. Mr. DeB.'s father was
concerned about his son's impulsive behavior and advised
him to go to his catchment area hospital for treatment.
Instead, Mr. DeB. stopped at the employment office and
was immediately hired.

During the course of his employment at the hospital
Mr. DeB. was also engaged in lucrative counterfeiting
operations, dealt profitably in stolen car parts, and
became an expert check forger, all offenses of which he
was later found not guilty by reason of insanity under
the then-operative Durham decision (1954).

Soon after his arrival on the ward as a patient,
Mr. DeB. made it clear that he wanted no part of what
limited treatment was being offered at the time (this
consisted of community meetings twice a week, group
therapy twice a week, chemotherapy, and individual con-
sultations with the ward psychiatrist around administrative issues on a daily basis as required). He preferred
to be by himself and resisted all approaches to him,
even threatening to file a writ of habeas corpus based
on the Fourth Amendment right against unlawful search
and seizure (in this case an inquiry by his psychiatrist
into his feelings). Mr. DeB.'s silence contrasted with
a sudden increase in the quantity and quality of writs
of habeas corpus filed by the patients on the ward.

The fact that many of the patients filing writs were
virtually illiterate and that the writs were written in
a very similar style pointed to Mr. DeB. as the initia-
tor of the activity. When asked about this, Mr. DeB.
readily admitted that he was serving as the patients'
lawyer and amanuensis and, in fact, took great pride in
this. It mattered little to him that much of the ward
psychiatrist's time for therapeutic interaction with patients was being spent in court at show-cause hearings,
and that other therapeutic activities, in an environment with limited resources, were being severely under-
mined. When confronted with the detrimental consequences
of his behavior, he seemed untouched and focused on what
he viewed as the psychiatrist's readiness to abrogate
his patients' legal rights.

Mr. DeB.'s behavior continued in this vein through
the psychiatrist's stay on the ward, and he carefully
documented all efforts on the staff's behalf to protect
the psychiatrist during violent altercations on the ward.
When queried as to why he was taking such copious notes,
the patient replied, "Well, we may be able to sue the
hospital for money damages some day, and if we don't

keep adequate records, we won't stand a chance in court.
You remember the <u>Williams</u> decision, don't you, Doctor?"

Case #2

Mr. B., a 22-year old male, was found guilty of the
possession of several illegal drugs, and was sent for
treatment of his drug habit to a local facility where he
had been known previously. Soon after he arrived, he
complained of withdrawal symptoms and insisted that a
physician be called. The staff on duty, which had had
extensive experience recognizing the symptoms of withdrawal from various addicting drugs, examined him and
felt that he was not in withdrawal but that this request was a manipulation. They felt that it would be
advisable to set limits on the patient's manipulative-
ness and refused to have a physician called. The patient, who came from a family of physicians, threatened
to sue the facility for damages, and used this incident
to ward off all attempts to treat him for his underlying problems. To all efforts to engage him he would
reply, "Look, even if I got in business with you guys,
you'll be shut down in a month anyway because of my
suit, so it's kind of useless, eh?" The staff in return
became embittered and withdrew from the patient. The
patient left the program against medical advice two
weeks later.

Discussion

The legal system provides a dramatic projective arena
for some impulse-ridden patients. Their inner struggles,
wishes, and fears find symbolic counterparts in judges, defendants, defense attorneys, witnesses, prosecutors, and the
litigation in which they engage. It is my contention that
very specific aspects of impulsive character structures find
displaced outlets in the law and in the claims of due process.
Unless lawyers and mental health professionals understand
this, much needless bitterness among them will result.

Two issues are involved here. The first concerns the
legal arena as one of controlled aggression. The rules are
reasonably clear, decorum is maintained, the actors have

their roles and titles--the courtroom has the flavor of a
set piece. To many persons overwhelmed by their own aggressive urges and consequent fears that they might murder or be
murdered, the courtroom promises control. My sense is that
Mr. DeB. (Case #1) was using his legal rights to express his
aggression in a controlled way, as well as to attempt to put
his therapist in as helpless a position as he may have felt
himself in. This latter use of the courtroom leads to the
second issue. The legal arena rightfully gives all participants an equal footing. Impulsive patients, who frequently
feel powerless, may use their legally enhanced powers to off-
set a chronic sense of powerlessness. Hospitals and doctors
may be seen as their usual tormentors, whom they now have
at a disadvantage.

This analysis, if correct, would suggest that psychiatrists might avoid many courtroom imbroglios if we perceived
them as ways in which these patients were coping with difficult aggressive feelings, and attempted to direct our work
with litigious patients to these issues. In my experience,
however, this is often not possible. For many of these patients, the need to project feelings is so great and the
process of forming a therapeutic alliance is often so difficult that the therapist's attempt to interpret behavior as
symptomatic of underlying fears and wishes often does not
succeed. Nonetheless, if we realize that court struggles on
the part of patients are often displacements, we may be able
to cope with them more effectively.

By definition, impulsive clients have difficulty with
control. It is often through the legal system that they
seek to reassert control over their lives and those of others
they feel they have lost. At a deeper level, this is a projection of the feared loss of inner control. The legal system exists to impose forced controls where voluntary ones
have failed and in this aspect the system and the patient
are perfect partners. In case #2, for example, Mr. B, having
been rebuffed in his efforts to manipulate the staff, may
have been fearing that he was going to lose direction over his
external and internal life. His threats to sue might have
represented his desperate attempts to regain autonomy.

Conclusion

Because the interface of law and psychiatry is so dependent on shifting definitions of illness, the sway of social
values, and the drift of judicial decisions, firm guidelines
are often illusory. I have tried to convey a sense of the
current state of the law in the areas covered, to give my
views on how we might best work within its guidelines, and to
suggest that mental health professionals retain the patient
as our primary focus in his and our interactions with the
judicial system.

References

Ayres, R. J., Jr., and Holbrook, J. T. 1975. Law, psycho-
    therapy, and the duty to warn: A tragic trilogy? Bay-
    lor Law Review, 27, 677-705.
Birnbaum, M. 1960. The right to treatment. Am. Bar Assoc.
    J., 46, 499-505.
Brakel, S. and Rock, R. 1971. The Mentally Disabled and the
    Law. Chicago: University of Chicago Press.
Burns, R. E. 1975. Tort law. Akron Law Rev., 9, 191-198.
Cal. Stats. 1974. Chapter 1534, at 4328.
Cleary, M. F. 1973. The Writ Writer. Am. J. Psychiat.,
    130, 319-322.
Covington v. Harris, 419 F. 2d 617 (D.C. Cir., 1969).
Curran, W. 1975. The right to psychiatric treatment: A
    "simple decision" in the Supreme Court. New Engl.
    J. Med., 293, 487-488.
Dershowitz, A. 1970. The law of dangerousness: Some fic-
    tions about predictions. J. Legal Ed., 23, 24-47.
Diamond, B. 1975. The psychiatric prediction of dangerous-
    ness. Univ. Pa. Law Rev., 123, 439-452.
Durham v. U.S., 1954. 214 F.2d 862.
Glassman, M. Torts. 1975. Cincinnati Law Rev., 44, 268-75.
Kaimowitz v. Dept. of Mental Health. Civil No. 73-19434-AW
    (Cir. Ct. of Wayne County, Michigan, filed July 10,
    1973).
Kaplan, R. 1975. Tarasoff v. Regents of the University
    of California: Psychotherapists, policemen and the
    duty of warn--an unreasonable extension of the common
    law? Golden Gate Univ. Law Rev., 6, 229-248.

Katz, J. 1969. The right to treatment--An enchanting legal
     fiction? Univ. of Chicago Law Rev., 36, 755-783.
Lake v. Cameron, 364 F. 2d 657 (D.C. Cir. 1966).
Liss, R. and Frances, A. 1975. Court-mandated treatment:
     Dilemmas for hospital psychiatry. Am. J. Psychiat.,
     132:9, 924-927.
Mass. Gen'l Laws, 1971. Chapter 123, Sections 1-38.
Mirakina, S. 1976. Tort law: California's extension of the
     duty to warn. Washburn Law J., 15, 496-502.
O'Connor v. Donaldson, 1974. F.2d 507.
Olmstead v. U.S., 1928.   277 U.S. 438, 479.
Patuxent Institution v. Daniels, 1966.   243 Md. 16, 221 A.
     2d., 397.
Rouse v. Cameron, 1966.   125 U.S. app. 366, 373 F. 2d 451.
Slovenko, R. 1973. Psychiatry and Law. Boston: Little,
     Brown and Co.
Stanley v. Georgia.   1969. 394 U.S. 557.
Tarasoff v. Regents of the University of California, 1974.
     13 Cal. 3d 177, 559 P.2d 553, 118 Cal. Rptr. 129.
Union Pacific v. Botsford, 1891.   141 U.S. 250, 251.
Valentine, G. 1975. Tarasoff v. Regents of the University
     of California: The psychotherapist's peril. Univ.
     Pittsburgh Law Rev., 37, 155-168.
Williams v. Robinson, 432 F. 2d 637, 642-43 (D.C. Cir. 1970).
Winters v. Miller, 446 F.2d 65 (2nd Cir. 1971).
Wyatt v. Stickney, 1972.   325 F. Supp 781, 1971; 334 F.
     Supp. 1341.
Zwerdling, Z. E. 1975. Informed consent and the mental pa-
     tient: California recognizes a mental patient's right
     to refuse psychosurgery and shock treatment. Santa
     Clara Lawyer, 15, 725-759.

Suggested Reading

Bazelon, D. 1974. The perils of wizardry. Am. J. Psychiat.,
     131:12, 317-322.
Halleck, S. L. 1974. Legal and ethical aspects of behavior
     control. Am. J. Psychiat. 131:4, 381-385.
Kopolow, L. A. 1976. A review of the major implications of
     the O'Connor v. Donaldson decision. Am. J. Psychiat.,
     133:4, 379-383.
McGarry, A. L. 1976. The holy legal war against state hos-
     pital psychiatry. N. Engl. J. Med., 294, 318-320.
Robitscher, J. 1972. Courts, state hospitals, and the right
     to treatment. Am. J. Psychiat., 129:3, 298-303.

Stone, A. 1976. Hanging the psychiatrists. Am. Bar Assoc.
    J., 62, 773-774.
Szasz, T. 1975. The danger of coercive psychiatry. Am.
    Bar Assoc. J., 61, 1246-1248.
Twerski, A. 1971. Treating the untreatable: A critique of
    the proposed right to treatment law. Hosp. Community
    Psychiatry, 22:9, 261-264.

PROBLEMS OF MENTAL HEALTH COUNSELING IN THE

CRIMINAL JUSTICE SYSTEM

Daniel H. Jacobs, M.D.

Director, Cambridge Court Clinic, and Instructor
in Psychiatry, Harvard Medical School at The
Cambridge Hospital, Cambridge, Massachusetts

The Eskimos have a word, Kulangeta, which means "his
mind knows what to do but he doesn't do it." It is used to
describe a man who repeatedly lies, cheats, or steals.
Kulangeta is not a behavior that the shamans or healers are
believed to be able to cure or change. When asked what would
have happened traditionally to such a person, an Eskimo re-
plies that someone would have pushed him off the ice when no
one was looking (Murphy, 1976).

Do mental health professionals really have anything
better to offer to those who commit antisocial acts than the
hands-off policy of the Eskimo shamans? Or should we yield
to those in our society who would deal with antisocial behavior by, if not a push off the ice, a push into the confinement of prison walls. This is the central question for
mental health professionals working in correctional institutions in general, and in state-supported court clinics in
particular, where outpatient evaluation and treatment of
offenders and their families is often undertaken. In Massachusetts, for example, staff in these court clinics saw
over 6500 offenders and their families in 1976 (Div. of
Legal Medicine, Mass. Dept. of Mental Health).

It is not only those working within the criminal justice
system who need be concerned with what, if anything, mental
health professionals can offer social deviants. More and
more violent, impulsive, and antisocial patients are appear-

145

ing in emergency rooms, outpatient clinics, and psychiatric
hospitals where they present difficult problems in treatment.
The question of what we can do to aid those with <u>Kulangeta</u>
becomes even more crucial when we realize that this year five
Americans in every hundred will be victims of some serious
crime, ranging from auto theft to murder. The number of
criminals imprisoned in our attempt to protect ourselves
has risen to over a quarter of a million (U.S. Dept. of
Justice Report, 1977).

What, other than the threat of punishment, can therapists offer in trying to dissuade persistent offenders from
antisocial behavior? Why should a delinquent high school
dropout stop stealing cars or breaking into homes? Why should
he give up the pleasures of immediate gratification to accept the new and sometimes unpleasant responsibilities of
a law-abiding citizen? We can tell him that his behavior is
destructive and may lead to prison. He, however, lives in
the present. The prospect of honest, menial labor is, for
him, as much an imprisonment as the local reformatory. The
real and imagined bars to his obtaining legally what television tells him every American should have seem as inflexi-
ble and confining as those of the county jail. The solitary
confinement that comes from perpetual distrust of others is,
at times, no greater than the loneliness of a state prison.

Offenders, furthermore, do not usually enter our courts
or prisons for a cure. They are in these institutions because they have come into conflict with the world around
them. Because their antisocial behavior is often egosyn-
tonic, they are not looking for help; they have simply been
caught. Why should offenders speak openly to "therapists"
in the criminal justice system--the representatives or em-
ployees of those with whom they are in conflict, part and
parcel of the wealth of this nation from which they often
feel excluded? What can the offender say to us "shamans"
that is not tinged with envy, longing, and rage?

If the persistent offender has difficulty in relating
to us and seeing our work as valuable, we may have an equally
difficult time committing ourselves to him. We are willing
to work, we say, but the offender isn't motivated. He often
does not consciously experience depression or anxiety (Vaillant, 1975), thus obviating the overt need for help. He
often does not keep appointments. He may substitute action,

drugs, or alcohol for understanding and feeling. Activity
and the immediate release of tension are his mode of dealing
with conflict, rather than insight and planning.

Even if the offender does keep his appointments, the
therapist may be faced with a sullen but passively compliant
patient who has no wish to participate in treatment or to
modify his behavior. Others may quite boldly try to use the
therapist for immediate gratification--to avoid prison,
obtain drugs, and so forth. These initial responses to the
treatment situation, while expected, are nevertheless extremely frustrating and are often injurious to professional
pride. We quickly recognize that the criminal often has a
marked fear of forming deep personal attachments and, as
Glover (1960) has pointed out, a penchant for disappointing
those who become attached to him.

The work is difficult and not always gratifying. Court
and prison personnel can, on the one hand, be too skeptical
of our efforts or, on the other, expect too much. Judges,
attorneys, and probation officers, burdened by overcrowded
dockets and huge caseloads, sometimes become impatient.
They want quick answers to hard questions. Is this person
dangerous? Should this adolescent be committed to a special
youth services division? Will this offender commit another
crime if freed? Often there is not a clear enough understanding that these questions cannot be answered after a
thirty-minute interview. Nor would we want them to be.
They are serious questions, and if we can answer them at all,
we can respond only after careful evaluation that sometimes
requires an extended period of time.

Continuing and more creative interchange among judges,
jailors, attorneys, and psychiatrists thus becomes necessary
and integral to the work of those involved in the criminal
justice system. In addition, the places where therapists
who treat offenders work--courts or prisons--are often geo-
graphically isolated, far from the professional supportive
world of hospitals or universities. Many workers experience
a sense of isolation and too few people with whom to exchange
information and ideas about their work. More formal connec-
tion between correctional centers--court clinics and insti-
tutions--and the staff of universities and teaching hospitals
in the area would help alleviate this problem.

If, despite these difficulties, mental health professionals choose to become involved in treating offenders,
then we must, in my opinion, become advocates for the offender. Such advocacy is not simple nor is it always popular.
I choose the word "advocate" because it comes closest to
connoting the active interest and understanding required.
It also implies an active sympathy for the offender, whatever his misdeeds. Aichhorn (1935) indicated this need for
understanding; for him the delinquent is always "right" in
his behavior, in the sense that he manages as best he can
and could not have behaved otherwise. We do not, after all,
condemn the patient with pneumonia for his cough. Although
we cannot in any way condone the offender's behavior, we need
to remain free of condemnation, often a barrier to the therapist's understanding.

If such active sympathy and advocacy can be achieved
by the therapist, it nonetheless raises particular problems
for those working within the criminal justice system. Where
does the therapist's allegiance ultimately lie? For those
working in prisons the problem is all but insurmountable:
it is difficult to serve the jailor and the jailed. Allegiance to the prisoner, on the one hand, invites (or augments)
difficulty with prison authorities sooner or later. Alliance with the authorities, on the other hand, makes difficult
or precludes winning the trust of inmates (Schmidelberg,
1960). Most therapists in the prison setting are caught in
the middle. Despite their best efforts, they usually have
neither the trust of the prisoners nor the authority to make
changes in the prison setting that would be therapeutic, or
at least more humane. Their position is often one of relative impotence, one quickly recognized by the prisoners whose
own feelings of impotence engender reluctance to ally themselves with those they view as the "weak sisters" of the
system.

Furthermore, to treat someone in so abnormal an environment as prison is questionable. With incarceration, anxiety
and sexual frustration increase. Existing abnormalities
and antisocial tendencies intensify. If we treat a patient
in so restricted and punitive an environment, we have little
way of knowing how he will adapt upon release, when he must
face issues and conflicts concerning liberty, family life or
its absence, employment, and the numerous hurts he is bound
to encounter. Furthermore, the usual therapist-patient rela-

tionship is severely compromised. The prisoner, like other
patients, but for better reasons, is always fearful he will
be judged rather than helped. Few in their right minds can
speak openly and honestly about their murderous wishes and
antisocial impulses to someone who might have the power to
recommend their continued if not indefinite incarceration.

I think treatment in most prisons should be limited to:
(1) crisis intervention with emphasis on helping the patient
adjust as best he can to the prison environment in which he
must live; (2) support and medication for psychotic or severely borderline patients; (3) insight-oriented therapy,
group or individual, for those prisoners interested, during
the last six to twelve months of their incarceration. Whenever possible, treatment should be continued by the same
therapist after discharge. Even such limited goals would
severely tax the prisons' mental health systems, and there
seems little hope that they can be met in the near future.

Our main emphasis should be on helping people before
they reach prison, or upon release. A surprising number of
offenders seek help on their own. A brief survey of patients
in one state court clinic indicated that over 50 percent of
the patients seen in treatment do not have therapy as a
condition of their probation. At least 25 percent of the
patients continue to come after probation has ended. Some,
however, seem to come only because they are forced to by the
judge. In addition to raising legal issues, at times such
enforced therapy has been considered unworkable by mental
health professionals. In general, we choose to see patients
who are motivated to change.

My own experience, however, suggests that enforced therapy can be effective. First, forcing the offender to come,
at least for an evaluation, provides an opportunity for the
therapist to try to engage him--an opportunity that might
otherwise be lost. The therapist must often use all his
skills in quickly finding a way to interest the offender
in continuing. Secondly, although many offenders, particularly adolescents, want desperately to talk with someone,
they cannot bring themselves to do it. They are afraid they
will be found crazy or labeled so by peers or relatives who
discover they are in treatment. If the court orders them
to seek help, they save face, declaring to others that they
are "forced" to go. In fact, many never miss an appointment

and benefit from treatment. Most delinquents and others on
probation know they will not be sent to jail for failing to
see the psychiatrist. They come with some, often unacknowledged, wish to be helped. Those who really don't want to
come, don't.

Many initially come to see the therapist as a way of
getting off the hook--avoiding jail, obtaining medicine, or
maybe even to steal something from the clinic. Often these
wishes for immediate gain are viewed by the therapist only
as manipulations or further proof of the patient's sociopathy. Fears of being "conned" by the patient may interfere with the therapist's understanding of these matters.
Too often professionals are afraid of being duped by the
offender or labeled a bleeding heart by colleagues. We
are quick to be suspicious of any secondary gain obtained
by the offender in seeing us. While such suspicions are
justified, they should not interfere too greatly with our
empathy. For that reason I do not bring to the clinic office
personal possessions with which I might not be willing to
part; too great a loss would interfere with my empathic
capacity. A balance in the therapist between active empathic involvement and assertive refusal to indulge destructive manipulation, as Wissler (1960) pointed out, is difficult to achieve but necessary for effective treatment. I
see the offender's attempt to stay out of jail, for instance,
as essentially healthy. It is the ego's attempt to adapt
to the painful reality of being caught--and I respect it.
As passivity is the greatest enemy of therapy and change, the
client's wish to change his circumstances, no matter how
manipulative or antisocial it first appears, is not unwelcome
by me. I can try to engage the patient around his wish.

Often the wishes of the offender cannot be granted.
When asked what they wanted for themselves, I don't know how
many delinquents reply with a smile, "A million dollars."
I cannot promise the offender that he will get what he wants,
but I do indicate we can work together toward it. While I
cannot provide the delinquent with a million dollars and the
immediate gratification of wishes it implies, I can agree
that it would be nice if we could find a way for him to get
some money for himself that didn't risk going to jail. In
fact, with all offenders, but particularly delinquents, I
try early in therapy to find something concrete that they
want for themselves that I can help them obtain--staying out
of prison, a job, helping to get a driver's license. In

some cases the patient refuses to tell me what he wants, or
simply doesn't know, or is too depressed to ask; then we
start there. How can we get to know what he wants?

I stress the specificity of the goal set initially for
several reasons. At the outset of therapy these patients
think concretely. This cognitive mode can be seen to serve
a defensive function that cannot be analyzed early in treatment but must be taken into account. Many of them, furthermore, have been deprived in some very real way. An abstract
interpretation or clarification in the face of realistic
concerns about employment, schooling, or health needs can
readily be seen by the offender as a further deprivation.
A pervasive and important fact we must not lose sight of is
that this population does have special needs which must be
recognized and addressed. Prompt diagnosis of these needs
and concern about their being met can help foster an alliance. Therapy that does not pay close attention to these
special needs is doomed to frustration.

My work in the court clinic of a medium-sized north-
eastern city made me especially aware of the needs of our
patients in the areas of education and health care. Of
178 adolescents screened in this clinic, 56 percent were
diagnosed as having learning disabilities, either by school
record or our own testing. Strong suggestions of learning
problems were found in another 28 percent, and further testing was indicated but not completed. Only 23 percent clearly
showed no learning disability. In another study, now under-
way, early data indicate that although the majority of
adolescents we see have average intelligence, they have
significant problems with auditory memory, sound recognition,
and sound blending. They also seem to have deficiencies in
gross motor coordination. Poor vision and absence of fully
coordinated eye movements are common. Such difficulties must
be carefully evaluated in terms of the patient's ability to
perform in school and their effect on his life and potential.
These crucial clinical findings emphasize the importance of
careful work with physicians, educators, and vocational
rehabilitation specialists as a large part of any meaningful
therapy within the criminal justice system.

In addition, these patients often have specific health
problems. Many need glasses and almost all require extensive
dental care. Their nutrition is poor. We have found that
these youths are surprisingly willing to talk about their

health needs. Part of a study conducted in our clinic provides for physical examinations of delinquents. We initially
thought it would be difficult for adolescents to consent to
an examination. They have been most agreeable. After learning of the proposed physical, some have begun to share with
the therapist their somatic concerns.

One of the frustrations we continually face is the pau-
city of educational and vocational programs, particularly
for the older adolescent. Where can one place an 18-year-old
high school dropout of dull normal intelligence, or one with
a perceptual problem, or one with a third-grade reading level
and a court record? Most often these individuals comprise
the growing ranks of the untrained, unwanted youth in our
highly specialized, industrialized society. In the particular court clinic referred to, we are fortunate to have the
services of an able tutor, provided by the city's school
department, who sees youths in the clinic and works to increase their skills. Through these efforts they can be
considered for what few vocational training programs are
available, or can at least pass the written test for the Army,
if they wish.

After the therapist has aligned himself with the client's
conscious wish to change some external circumstance and has
demonstrated his willingness to help the client with some
special need, the analysis of the patient's character problems and the ways in which they interfere with achieving his
stated goals may begin. One patient, who assaulted a shop-
keeper, was a highly intelligent but lonely, isolated man
who never recovered from the death of his mother when he was
a child. He despaired of his life and his future, claiming
that having only a high school diploma limited him terribly.
He could not tolerate menial or manual work for which he was,
in fact, ill suited. When I referred him to the state rehabilitation commission, which offered him money for further
education, he resisted further involvement. This resistance
to concrete assistance could then be subject to scrutiny.
His underlying conviction that nothing could change became
verbalized. He could trust no one and was, ultimately, afraid
of being disappointed and hurt again as he had been in his
childhood. After several months of work together, he was
able to enroll in school.

The delinquent who wants a million dollars must see
how he fears fulfilling even the smallest wish--one we are

willing to help him with, much less a million-dollar one.
He clings to the impossible dream in part in order to avoid
facing up to the real barriers to success within him. Others
claim they want help in staying out of prison, but when a
plan is outlined with them they fail to follow it. The
dichotomy between the genuine conscious wishes of these
clients and their actions can be clarified for them by the
therapist, thus bringing the problem into the treatment situation.

This dichotomy between wishes and deeds, when pointed
out, often leads the patient to feelings of frustration or
anger, and such feelings may threaten continued treatment.
The client may try to relieve the frustration through immediate action of an antisocial nature or by fleeing treatment.
Treatment therefore must be modified to the psychological
and practical needs of these patients, who are often highly
ambivalent and unstable. It is extremely important that in
addition to kindly confrontation, the therapist provide
support and alternative ways of handling problems. It is
important, for instance, to interpret the patient's hostility
so that it is not felt as a reproach and, whenever possible,
to give full acknowledgment to good, generous impulses. I am
careful to avoid remarks that may make the client too anxious.
I remain very real to the patient and involved. Later in
treatment I may become more reserved and begin working with
transference material, but only after a solid alliance has
been built which will help me aid the patient in tolerating
the rage and longings he may begin to focus on me.

At every phase of this work the question of confidentiality arises. We can expect that many of our clients will
continue some form of antisocial behavior after their treatment begins. We are lucky if an offender shares what he is
doing with us. If he happens to commit a felony, it should,
according to the law, be reported to the authorities. If
the therapist does not report antisocial behavior in order
to prevent rupturing the alliance, he may be in the uncomfortable position of being regaled with stories of antisocial behavior which his treatment is meant to prevent. In
addition, if the judge, probation officer, or warden finds
out that the therapist has listened to such stories without
reporting them, the latter endangers his working relationship with others in the system. Of even greater concern is
the possibility that some innocent person might be hurt.

No easy resolution of these conflicting treatment aspects exists. One can avoid the conflicts to some extent by being clear in one's own mind and with the patient about one's moral and professional obligation. I work within the criminal justice system as a therapist, not a detective, police officer, or judge. My first obligation, therefore, is to the client and his best interests. When the offender begins treatment, I indicate that nothing detrimental will be told to the court unless his actions are such that he seems likely to physically harm himself or others. I tell him that if he tells me he has, immediately prior to or during the treatment, seriously hurt someone, I will require him to surrender himself, or will report the occurrence myself. If during the course of treatment he feels he is likely to harm someone and is worried about it, voluntary hospitalization is preferable to prison, and I will help arrange such hospitalization for him. I always indicate I am sympathetic with his wishes to remain free and will try to help him in that regard, but he must also help himself. I also indicate that should he get into trouble and be caught while in treatment, I will feel badly, as a prison sentence would interrupt the progress he is making (or has shown the willingness to make), but he should not expect that I will plead his case in court. These clarifications are easier for the client to accept when he recognizes that you are or have been genuinely helpful in other areas--education, physical health, or encouraging the court to consider probation rather than prison.

If the offender is on probation with a specific condition that he be in treatment, I tell him that my obligation is to report two or more successive absences to his probation officer. I explain that I do not know how his probation officer or the court will handle these absences--they might well do nothing--but that is between the defendant and the court. I promise that if the court requests information about his treatment, we will discuss together what is appropriate to reveal. I always offer to let the client read the report before it is sent, and I try to keep the information sent to the court minimal.

For evaluation that the court requests, such as aid in sentencing, I tell the client from the outset the purpose of our meetings in terms of the court's request; but I add that there may be other concerns that he has that he also might want to discuss during our meetings. I let him know that I will give information and clinical opinions only on

the issue which the court has requested. Furthermore, I will
discuss my report with him before it is sent to the judge so
he may have a chance to comment on its contents. I make it
clear that there is room in my thinking for modification of
the report if the patient can point out how I have erred
in my evaluation. In so doing, I not only clarify my role,
but also offer the offender a chance to actively participate
in the evaluation. This is particularly important for a
patient population likely to externalize problems and feel
acted upon. I try as much as possible in these explanations
to use the word "we" to foster the idea of an alliance, of
working together, and of shared responsibility for the results. I also indicate that I personally do not believe
imprisonment is usually the best answer to problems and that,
if possible, we will try to find alternatives. I make it
clear to the offender that while I am willing to work with
him to find alternatives, all judgments and dispositions
will be made by the court.

If, as has happened several times after a lengthy evaluation period or the beginning of treatment, a man is sent
to prison despite my recommendations that he be placed on
probation, I keep in touch with the prisoner, usually by
mail, offering to see him upon release. This can be important to a man who feels abandoned behind prison walls. Of
the three cases in which I was involved, all continued their
treatment upon release.

Patients I see in the state court clinic described are
often products of persistent exclusion that began long before they became deviant--exclusion from stable family life
and an adequate "holding environment," and from effective
education and economic opportunity. The quality of their
lives prior to appearances in court clearly must be our larger
concern. Counseling within the criminal justice system offers too little, too late. We can try to help an offender
better his self-esteem and improve his impulse control.
We cannot counsel him to respect himself when society clearly has not accepted him or provided adequately for him.
Our highly technical age provides less and less opportunity
for the slow learner, too few vocational programs for the
young adult, and too few jobs to prepare for. Counseling
within the criminal justice system can be a worthwhile beginning but, in the long run, the larger society must provide the numerous support systems that help to prevent crime
and are necessary for true rehabilitation.

References

Aichhorn, A. 1935. Wayward Youth. New York: Meridian.

Commonwealth of Massachusetts. Statistical Report. 1976.
    Division of Legal Medicine, Dept. of Mental Health.

Eissler, K. 1949. General Problems of Delinquency, Search-
    lights on Delinquency, International Universities Press,
    pp. 3-25.

Glover, E. 1960. The Roots of Crime. New York: Interna-
    tional Universities Press.

Murphy, J.M. 1976. Psychiatric labelling in crosscultural
    perspective, Science, 191, 1019-1028.

Schmidelberg, M. 1949. The analytic treatment of major
    criminals: Therapeutic results and technical problems.
    Searchlights on Delinquency. New York: International
    Universities Press, 174-189.

U.S. Dept. of Justice, Law Enforcement Admin. Assistance,
    Natl. Criminal Justice Info. and Stat. Serv., 1977.
    Prisoners in state and federal institutions on Decem-
    ber 31, 1976, No. SD-NPS-PSF GH.

Valliant, G.E. 1975. Sociopathy as a human process. Arch.
    General Psychiatry, 32, 178-183.

THE HOMICIDAL PATIENT

Stanley I. Kruger, Ph.D.

Massachusetts Department of Correction

My original charge for this paper was to describe how the potentially homicidal patient can be recognized. My response to that task is that it cannot be done. Perhaps we can talk about people who might kill someone or could kill someone, but we cannot predict this behavior in an individual case. Moreover, we have great difficulty assessing "dangerousness," the necessity for "involuntary commitment," "mental illness diagnoses," and "being in need of care and treatment" with any degree of reliability. In fact, in reviewing the psychiatric literature, two lawyers (Ennis and Litwack, 1974) concluded that little evidence exists that psychiatrists are any more expert than lay persons in making these predictions. Yet the courts and the law assume that psychiatrists can reach reliable and valid conclusions concerning these questions, which have awesome implications for the lives of the patients being evaluated, such as: Should they be free persons? Should they be involuntarily held? Should they be tried for offenses and perhaps sent to prison?

I shall briefly review some of the articles Ennis and Litwak refer to because they address the issue of predicting behavior, especially dangerous behavior. In one paper, Steadman and Keveler (1972) report their findings pursuant to the Baxstrom v. Herold decision. In this case the New York State Supreme Court held that 969 prisoner-patients who remained in the New York Department of Corrections hospitals after their prison terms had expired must be released and committed civilly, if at all. Each of these patients had been adjudged mentally ill and too dangerous for release or transfer to civil hospitals. One year after the patients were transferred to civil hospitals, 147 had been discharged to the community

and 702, while still in civil hospitals, were found to present "no special problems to the hospital staff." Only 7
(from the original group of 969) were so difficult or dangerous that recommitment to a Department of Corrections
hospital was required. (Throughout this study, 113 of the
original group of 969 could not be traced for follow-up.) In
a further follow-up of the same population, after four years,
27 percent of the patients were living in the community,
less than 1 percent of the individuals had been convicted of
a crime (only 2 of the 9 for felonies), and 3 percent were in
a correctional facility or hospital for the criminally insane.

In another paper describing a situation at a state treatment center for sexually dangerous persons, Kozol, et al.
(1972) tell of 49 patients who were considered dangerous by
a team of at least five mental health professionals and who
were released by the Court after a hearing, contrary to the
recommendation of the professionals. Of that group of 49,
65 percent had not been found to have committed a violent
crime within five years of return to their community.

Clearly, the vast majority of the patients cited in these
studies did not require maximum security, and a very small
percentage proved to be dangerous at all. On the one hand,
this would indicate a tendency to overpredict violence and
dangerousness. One could speculate that this occurs in part
because we get no feedback from patients erroneously labeled
"dangerous"; they are locked up and cannot prove the error
of the label. On the other hand, if we err and call someone
nondangerous who proves in fact to be dangerous, we learn
about it with great impact and often with considerable pub-
licity. The tendency is then to err, if we must, in a con-
servative direction and to categorize more people as dangerous than is necessary. Further, professionals, like most
people, have strong feelings about violence, dangerousness,
murder--and these feelings influence their responses to persons so labeled. (We will discuss this issue later when we
talk about countertransference in working with violent and
homicidal persons.)

Ennis and Litwack cite study after study demonstrating
excessive prediction of dangerousness and violence. The
point, I think, is clear--we cannot predict who will do violence and/or who will murder.

Who, then, are the homicidal persons that I am discussing? The Massachusetts Department of Correction published an analysis of all murderers convicted in the Commonwealth between the years 1943 and 1966 (Carney, et al., 1963). The 238 subjects in this group were compared with the samples used in base expectancy studies; all subjects committed to the Department of Correction in 1965 provided additional comparative data.

In summary, murderers were found to be different from other criminals in several ways. Women were underrepresented in the murder group; only 1 in 50 of the murderers was female, while about 1 in 5 of the other offenders was a woman. Murderers were more likely to have been single; of the 114 murderers who were married, 30 percent were widowed while only 4.3 percent of the other offenders were widowed. (In a sense, this is a spurious finding since of the 35 convicted murderers who were widowed, 29 or 82.9 percent, were committed for killing their spouses.)

Murderers were underrepresented in the lower occupational class and were overrepresented in the middle occupational class and student categories. Regarding alcohol or drug abuse, they also showed significantly lower symptoms of problem drinking (indicated by two or more arrests for drunkenness) or narcotics addiction (indicated by one or more arrests for narcotics offenses).

Further, murderers tended to be older at their first arrest, and the proportion of those with six or more prior arrests was almost twice as high in the other offender sample (64.4 percent) as it was in the sample of convicted murderers (34.4 percent). (This difference was significant at the .001 level of confidence.) Further still, two out of three in the murderer group had never been arrested for drunkenness and only 1 (!) of the 238 convicted murderers had a prior narcotics arrest.

Over half the convicted murders (55.5 percent) had no prior commitments in an adult correctional institution, while only 29.9 percent of the other offenders had no prior commitments. Convicted murderers' families tended to maintain a rather high degree of interest; 82 percent had at least a sustained interest from their families. Only 12.1 percent appeared to be isolated from their families or had no living

relatives. Murderers present very few disciplinary problems
in the institution; 89 percent had fewer than five reports
and 42 percent had none at all. This is particularly impres-
sive when one considers that they spend long periods in the
institution.

The description for "murderer" resulting from this analysis then becomes: a male who is older than other offenders
at the time of his first arrest, has fewer prior arrests,
has an interested family, and neither gets boisterous when
drinking (if he drinks), nor gets caught using narcotics (if
he uses them). Upon returning to the community (and 71 subjects had returned), their recidivism rate was 10.3 percent
as compared to 59.5 percent for the other inmates. (One of
those released was arrested for first-degree murder. Seven
others were returned--2 for assault and battery, 3 for
larceny, 1 for illegal possession of a firearm, and 1 for
driving without a license; 4 of the 71 released were women
and none of them had any further arrests.)

Now that we have an overview of what a murderer may be
like, let us look at some individuals who represent groups
or types of murderers. "Joe" might be classified as a pro-
fessional--in prison argot, a "hit man." In prison for illegal possession of a weapon, Joe has never been convicted of
murder, but the police feel they know that he has killed at
least half a dozen persons. He allegedly is employed by a
group for use as an "enforcer," achieving the aims of his
employer through threat or violence, and, when needed, as an
executioner. He is in his late thirties, soft-spoken, articulate, and very bright. He is respected in the community.
Other inmates defer to him, giving him a wide berth. He
tends to stay by himself, has few friends, and those with
whom he associates are usually high in the hierarchy of his
group. The officers too tend to treat him with respect, and
he in turn treats them respectfully. He does not get into
institutional trouble, and probably helps to keep the institution quiet. He may be in a little side business but rarely
does illegal things himself; he probably has a group of under-
lings who do his bidding. He does not want excitement or
upset and actually has an interest in the place being order-
ly. Because he may be involved indirectly in some of the
gambling or pill traffic, he does not want the administrative
enforcement group to become anxious and clamp down; that would
interfere with his "action." Consequently, he polices the
place via his men so that the institution appears quiet.

People like Joe are not often apprehended for their
homicides, nor do they seek psychological assistance if they
are in prison. They are businessmen, part of whose job is
to kill people, and they do their business well. They plan
their work carefully, often study the intended victim, and
set the time and place for the deed so that it will provide
minimum risk to themselves with maximum chance for success.
They are not impulsive, they control their feelings well,
and they appear remarkably free of guilt. Moreover, their
behavior is rewarded in their own subculture, and they are
looked upon as respected, even distinguished, citizens; they
are the cream of the group, so to speak. This is not to
say that they do not have problems. Harrassment by law enforcement groups, occasional trips to prisons, and threats
from the enforcement arm of other groups are all realities.
But they are viewed by individuals like Joe as occupational
hazards to be tolerated or dealt with appropriately. Their
families tend to be stable. They often are married and have
children whom they protect and shelter. Real involvement and
caring relationships with these people seem to exist over
long periods of time. As a matter of fact, with the exception of their area of specialty, that is, killing, they might
be regarded as "normal" business persons, subject to similar
stresses of both life and business and often resolving them
in similar ways. It may be that I am understating the degree
of pathology, for, in fact, one rarely gets to know any of
this type of murderer really well. The general impression
created, however, is of a relatively stable, confident, con-
flict-free individual.

No such feeling of well being emanates from other types
of homicidal persons. Most of them evince great difficulty
in dealing with angry feelings. Impulsive outbursts and
memories of sadistic acts are often part of their history.
Torturing of animals, memories of being severely punished or
tortured themselves, being set upon by authority figures,
constantly harrassed, feeling misunderstood and resenting all
these perceived mistreatments, and being unable to retaliate
because one is too small, or too weak, or too inadequate, or
too unimportant--all these kinds of acts and feelings fill
their recollections. Sometimes the resentment remains dormant
for long periods, or it is suppressed until it is beyond en-
durance and then the blow-up occurs. Sometimes, as one of
these persons grows to adolescence and adulthood, the determination is made that one will tolerate such mistreatment no

more, and every slight or injury, real or fancied, leads to
retaliation, sometimes massive in nature, sometimes culminating in murder. Such was the case in which a professional
man was involved in a rear-end collision with one of these
perpetually angry persons. From accounts of witnesses, the
first party got out to exchange credentials and was attacked
and killed by the driver of the other car.

"Herb" was not like one of these persons. He was raised
in a middle-class family by two aunts and his mother, who was
an alcoholic; his father had died when he was quite young.
The women raised him to be a "perfect gentleman," and in fact
he became quite successful, graduated from college, and by the
age of 30 held a responsible job with a large commercial
organization. He was mildly effeminate in manner and had
difficulty in relating to women except in a "buddy" manner.
He perceived his mother as controlling, domineering, and someone to whom he could not stand up. He felt he had no effective way of dealing with her and could only keep his resent-
ments bottled up inside himself. Meanwhile, she became pro-
gressively more addicted to alcohol and behaved in a quite
unreasonable and provocative way. For example, she once sold
the house they lived in together while he was away briefly
on a business trip.

On returning from another business trip, Herb found
himself barred from his own home by a bolted door and locked
windows. He recalled knocking at the door for a long time,
then looking in through a small glass pane and seeing his
mother on the floor, passed out. As he continued banging
at the door, he recalled feeling his anger increase. His
mother finally roused herself and stumbled to the door, un-
locking it. Herb burst in past her. She was wearing only a
dressing gown, partly undone and held together with a sash.
He turned around to talk with her and saw her walking down
the steps to the street. He ran after her, grabbed her, and
dragged her back into the house, asking her where she thought
she was going. She told him she had a date in the local bar
with a male friend and struggled to get free so that she
might leave. At this point Herb blacked out momentarily, but
he apparently took the sash and knotted it around her neck,
strangling her. He does not remember doing this, but does
recall the thought, "I guess that ties up the package," passing through his mind. Then he cooked supper for them both.
When he went to look for his mother, he found her lying on the

floor, dead, recalled what had occurred, removed the sash,
tried artificial respiration, and when that failed, called
the police.

Herb became seriously depressed after coming to prison,
and developed thoughts and preoccupations about his mother.
For example, if it were snowing, he might think, "I wonder if
Mother is cold." His formulation when he was feeling better
was, "It was like a dam burst," and all the years of domina-
tion and the attendant bitterness and resentment came pour-
ing forth in that one act. Parenthetically, he confided that
if he had not been sent to prison, he would have had to kill
himself.

"Len" was an entirely different sort of person. He had
been on his own since the age of 16 when his mother had died
and "they just forgot about me." He had ten siblings and,
according to Len, no relative volunteered to care for him.
He was about 38 years old when seen as a murderer. He had
been committed previously to the treatment facility for sexually dangerous persons with multiple sex offenses against
children. None of the children with whom he had been involved had been seriously physically injured. He related all
his problems up to the time of his mother's death, remembered
her funeral, touching her in the coffin, and "feeling like
a darkness descend over his head." He talked about feelings
of loneliness and homesickness, of never belonging anyplace,
and about his anger at God for taking his mother from him.

Len was released from the treatment center at age 28 by
court order. Shortly after his release from incarceration,
he killed a five-year-old boy. He recounted the murder and
the day preceding it. He had gotten day work in a construc-
tion job, had planned to go to work but didn't because voices
told him to stay in his room. He recalled having "funny
thoughts," the desire to kill something, first wanting to
kill a dog but none was available. The night before the
crime he recalled sitting alone in his room, feeling very
lonely, looking at himself in the mirror, watching himself
drinking beer. He described this time and the days before as
"dark days" when he drank a lot, sometimes with a fellow
worker, then alone, always feeling very lonely. He went to
sleep, got up early, and drank some more beer. The victim
just happened to be passing by. Len called him over, pulled
him through the window, strangled him, and then sexually

assaulted him. He said that after he killed the boy, it was
"like the darkness lifted." He then went to the police and
reported the offense. At one point after commitment, he
attempted suicide. At various times in prison Len has been
overtly and blatantly psychotic--hearing voices talking to
him, having outside persons control his thoughts, and so
forth. During other periods, he has adjusted well to the institution.

As is evident from the case material presented, homicidal males come in many different garbs, from successful
businessmen-type hit men and impulsive, angry persons with
character disorders, to those with borderline or perhaps psychotic personalities. Some have been able to isolate the
affective response to this most distressing crime so effectively that it can be dispatched by a simple catch phrase.
By so doing, it loses its impact upon and meaning to the
perpetrator. It is a way of controlling, after a time, what
must have been intense and overwhelming feelings. Perhaps,
too, such phrases serve to control associated responses too
threatening to deal with. Let us look at "Frank" in this regard.

Frank had been in the armed services during World War
II. For no reason that he can think of, one day he took an
axe and hit a fellow worker in the head with it, killing him.
When asked for a reason, he says, "It was just one of those
spur-of-the-moment things." When asked whether it would have
been the same if another person had been there, he says he
can't tell..."It was just one of those spur-of-the-moment
things."

Frank was found not guilty by reason of insanity. He
was placed in a mental hospital and following discharge was
transferred to an inpatient V.A. facility where he spent some
time. Then he was placed on outpatient status and followed
for almost a year before being discharged. Five months later,
while at home, for no apparent reason, Frank removed a hammer
from a nail in the storage area where it was hanging and
killed his father-in-law. When I saw him about thirteen
years after this murder, he could describe vividly where the
other family members were and what they were doing when he
committed the murder. He denied that the act was related to
any feeling of resentment or anger and described himself as
getting on well with the victim--eating with him, chatting
with him at times, and generally feeling good about him.

When asked why the murder occurred, he could only explain
that "it was just one of those things."

Finally, there is the type of murderer who kills someone
in the course of committing another offense. "Henry" is one
of these. He was an unemployed laborer who had a wife and
small child, and came from a low-income area where poverty
was an everyday reality. He had lost his previous job through
no fault of his own and was disappointed and bitter toward the
world. He felt himself belittled by the system each time he
had to sign for a check. His wife tried to be supportive,
telling him that things would work out, and that he should
keep trying. But he described himself at the time as feeling like "not a man."

Henry had been involved in crime before. He had a juvenile record for breaking into places to steal and also a
conviction for a serious assault. He felt he had to do something about his painful economic reality and decided to break
into a house to steal. But he did something unusual for him
at this point--he bought a pistol. Henry has never been
able to explain this to himself, for although he maintained
that he only wanted to steal, he did in fact take the gun
with him. He broke into a house in a middle-class neighborhood and proceeded to search for things of worth. He had
thought that the people were away on vacation and that the
house would be empty. In his ransacking, however, he entered
the bedroom where the couple who owned the home were asleep.
The woman was awakened and, perceiving a man standing in the
doorway of her darkened bedroom, started to scream. Henry
panicked and fired toward the noise, emptying his gun into
the darkened room. He then fled empty-handed and was apprehended shortly thereafter. Both the woman and her husband
were killed by the shots. This "incidental" kind of killing
is often blamed on the victim by the killer with such phrases
as, "If he hadn't moved, I wouldn't have killed him," or "If
she hadn't screamed, I wouldn't have shot," or "If he hadn't
reached for his gun, I wouldn't have had to fire." These
responses provide some insight into the projective mechanism
often seen in working with these people, as well as their
feelings of entitlement and their misperception of reality.
It is as if they were correct and had a "right" to be there,
and that the victim was at fault for the killing.

Let me return briefly to the question of murderer pre-
dictability and consider what might be done about the issues

of recognizing potential killers and then treating them.
Someone like Joe is particularly difficult to spot unless you
know him personally. He often looks and behaves like most
other people, is unconflicted about his work, and indeed
would deny that he ever was involved in any such activity. He
wants nothing from a therapeutic relationship, feels little
psychological pain, and would not share it even if he did because that would make him vulnerable. He does not trust
people generally, relates closely only to a very few, and
holds his own counsel.

The angry unnamed killer (the second party in the auto ac
cident referred to; let's call him Bill) is somewhat easier to
identify. He probably has a history of impulsive and/or explosive behavior. He walks around with a chip on his shoulder, and persons like him can often be found in local bars with
the reputation of fighter, or in prison with the label "nut."
Whether or not he kills is coincidental to the circumstances
of any confrontation. For example: Is Bill carrying a knife
today? Is the other guy big enough and able to defend himself? Has Bill had a couple of drinks to further impair his
faulty judgment? Is there another deadly weapon at hand like
a crowbar? With Bill, life or death depends upon such circumstances. He may become involved in treatment if he is
hurting enough. Prison is a difficult place and places considerable stress on fellows like Bill. Their usual motoric
modes of expression are shut off; they are often surrounded
by other tough men, some of whom are almost as willing to
fight as they; and the specter of prolonged incarceration
weighs particularly heavy on them. Many of them become depressed and do in fact seek aid. The therapeutic task is
to build in a time delay, however brief, between the impulse
and the act. If one can achieve this and get Bill to consider the implication of his act, Bill can really be helped.
Also, just simple aging tends to slow down the Bills among us
and may be the greatest ally in their habilitation.

Herb, the mother-killer, is difficult to identify before
the fact, as are the rest, but the chances are excellent that
he will never be placed in a circumstance where such extreme
behavior is likely again. He is an excellent release risk
because his crime is so specific to the relationship with the
murdered person, and the likelihood that the same stresses
will occur again are quite small. Herb, if he should become
involved in treatment, would need to consider alternate acceptable modes for venting his hostility and aggression.

Len, the sex offender who killed the five-year-old child, needed a relationship. Clearly the issue for him was loneliness, and the theme of desertion by the mother is repeated by the judge who ordered his release. The murder might have been averted if he had had someone to talk with, to visit, with whom to share the overwhelming burden of the loneliness as he sat alone the night before the murder drinking beer and staring at himself in the mirror. A continuing therapeutic relationship could prove very useful in helping persons like Len who are sad, friendless isolates without the comfort or support of meaningful relationships. With support and success experiences, some of them could become useful citizens.

Frank, for whom murder was "just one of those things," is very difficult to evaluate retrospectively. Corrections therapists see him many years after the deed, when all the feelings have been bottled up and stored away with the catch-phrase. Frank does not want to examine those feelings and we have no way of knowing now why the two murders occurred. Without this knowledge, we have no way of evaluating the likelihood of another occurrence of homicide. However, time has passed--more than thirteen years in his case. Is he still dangerous? Should the community take the risk of another killing? Who is to say?

Henry, our last murderer, is difficult to identify in isolation from his primary offense. If he is carrying a weapon, he is more likely to kill than if not. If he is going into a confrontational situation, like robbing a bank during the day, he is more likely to kill than if he is breaking into vacant buildings. With this type of murderer, consideration of why it is necessary to carry the weapon and whether or not there might not be more fruitful ways of being manly or successful sometimes can have quite beneficial results. Many of these persons are quite social, like to talk, and can become easily involved in therapeutic activities.

Working effectively in psychotherapy with an inmate who has murdered raises, of necessity, distressing feelings in the therapist, such as fear, disgust, anxiety, and general discomfort concerning issues of violence. The act of murder provokes fantasies of further uncontrollable outbursts, bloody rooms, victims screaming--perhaps with the therapist as victim. One consequence for the professional who is simul-

taneously troubled by these fantasies **and** is seeking to help
the inmate patient, the institution, and the community may
be the avoidance of pertinent diagnostic issues. The therapist may not, for example, facilitate the inmate's telling
of his own story. One inmate at a state prison claimed he
had been there for several years and no one had asked or
permitted him to talk of his offense. In this case there may
have been concern that certain questions would trigger and
provoke an outburst, wherein the patient would turn on the
examiner. Or the evaluator or therapist dealing with a murderer, more than other types of criminals, may not be able
to confront his own feelings about the crime, or some quality
of the crime which he finds particularly repugnant--if, for
example, the victim was a child and the clinician has a child
of the same age. Or the clinician, notably humane on a conscious level, may have unconscious feelings about murder which
he cannot deal with and must push away.

Unless the diagnostician-clinician-therapist is aware
of his own responses and thoughts and feelings and is able
to deal with these, he will be unable to deal adequately with
the homicidal patient. His own defenses may blind him to
the facts. He may shut off valuable sources of information;
or he may label the person "psychotic" or "untreatable" to
get rid of him. Or he may consciously avoid dealing with
important issues around aggression, for example, because he
is concerned that he may provoke an outburst; in fact, though,
the careful, calm eliciting of events in great detail is needed so that pertinent judgments can be made.

Clearly, these countertransference issues need to be
dealt with in some way. Although with junior staff this
is a supervisory issue, the feelings we have been discussing
do not respect seniority and sometimes occur in older, sea-
soned clinicians. It may be helpful to arrange a small
seminar or group where staff working with the patient who
has killed can get together and discuss their feelings, judgments, and approaches with colleagues who share similar experiences. Experienced clinicians can get considerable support, insight, and even training from small peer groups where
they learn to feel comfortable with the other members.

Long-term psychotherapeutic relationships with homicidal patients present all the problems discussed, in addition to problems of working with impulsive personalities,

usually in a controlled setting where the patient will be
or has been retained for a long period of time. An early
issue for the murderer is the feeling of hopelessness at being incarcerated in a hospital or prison; hesitancy in talking about the crime or related experiences follows fairly
closely. In part this arises from his usual mistrust and
suspiciousness of the therapist, who is seen as being a member of the establishment. But part of this hesitancy bespeaks
an unwillingness in many murderers to reawaken the memories
and feelings of what, for most of them, was a painful and
negative experience. It is probably best not to push for information too early in a therapeutic relationship, although
this may be necessary in a diagnostic circumstance. The
therapist should be willing to be active if necessary. These
patients usually see this as helpful if they become blocked
and if the anxiety level is kept manageable.

Defining limits clearly via a contract and structure is
useful in setting boundaries for both the patient and the
therapist. The therapeutic contract arrived at should include
confidentiality and its limits, time and place of meeting,
what kinds of intervention, if any, the therapist will employ, and other circumstances and limits that appear necessary.

The clear structuring of the therapeutic circumstance is
helpful both to the patient and therapist for several reasons. It provides a context for their relationship where both
know what is to be expected. It removes some of the threat
of the unknown and defines what demands each can make of the
other. It permits both to become a bit more comfortable so
that they can get to know each other and work together.
And, hopefully, it ultimately makes possible therapeutic
change.

Each individual must be treated in the context of his
own psychological issues. There is no generalizable therapy
for homicidal patients, just as there is no generalizable
predictor of this most violent behavior. However, with careful case evaluation, treatment planning, and goal setting,
meaningful assistance can be given to many homicidal patients
who are willing to participate.

References

Carney, F., Tosti, A. and Turchette, A. 1968. An analysis of convicted murderers in Massachusetts: 1943-1966. Publication of the Massachusetts Department of Correction, No. 983.

Ennis, B., and Litwack, R. 1974. Psychiatry and the presumption of expertise: Flipping coins in the courtroom. Calif. Law Rev., 62, 693-752.

Kozol, H., Boucher, R., and Garofalo, R. 1972. The diagnosis and treatment of dangerousness. Crime and Delinquency, 18, 371-392.

Steadman, H., and Keveles, G. 1972. The community adjustment and criminal activity of the Boxstrom patients: 1966-70. Am. J. Psychiat., 129, 304-310.

Part IV

Historical Overview and Future Issues

HISTORICAL OVERVIEW: FORE AND AFT

John E. Mack, M.D.

Professor of Psychiatry, Harvard Medical School
at The Cambridge Hospital, Cambridge, Massachusetts

When one considers the dimensions of the problem of impulsive individuals, it is remarkable how late in our history the mental health professions began to give serious attention to their study. I would like to consider some of the reasons why we have been so tardy in focusing our efforts in this area.

The psychiatry of the eighteenth century was primarily the psychiatry of "unreason"; in simple terms, patients were mainly individuals who had lost their reason. Although the social context may determine what problems are considered matters of impulse control (an impulse disorder in one culture may be characterized as a life style in another social milieu), cases that we now clearly place in this category were recognized as early as 1800, particularly by Philippe Pinel (1962). Despite changes or shifts in the value/belief system of Western culture—and the medical diagnostic classification arising therefrom—these cases are, at least in part, quite recognizable and similar to those that we see now. The following is the first description in the literature familiar to me that describes a patient with an impulse disorder. Pinel writes:

> The following relation will place in a conspicuous point of view, the influence of a neglected or ill directed education, in inducing upon a mind naturally perverse and unruly, the first symptoms of this species of mania.

Pinel called this disorder "mania sans délire"—mania without delirium or without loss of reason. He continued:

173

The only son of a weak and indulgent mother [the patient] was encouraged in the gratification of every caprice and passion, of which an untutored and violent temper was susceptible. The impetuosity of his disposition increased with his years. The money with which he was lavishly supplied removed every obstacle to his wild desires. Every instance of opposition or resistance, roused him to acts of fury. He assaulted his adversary with the audacity of a savage; sought to reign by force, and was perpetually embroiled in disputes and quarrels. If a dog, a horse, or any other animal offended him, he instantly put it to death. If ever he went to a fête or any other public meeting, he was sure to excite such tumults and quarrels, as terminated in actual pugilistic encounters, and he generally left the scene with a bloody nose. This wayward youth, however, when unmoved by passions, possessed a perfectly sound judgement. When he came of age, he succeeded to the possession of an extensive domain. He proved himself fully competent to the management of his estate, as well as to the discharge of his relative duties, and he even distinguished himself by acts of beneficence and compassion. Wounds, law-suits, and pecuniary compensations, were generally the consequences of his unhappy propensity to quarrel. But an act of notoriety put an end to his career of violence. Enraged at a woman who had used offensive language to him, he precipitated her into a well. Prosecution was commenced against him, and on the deposition of a great many witnesses, who gave evidence to his furious deportment, he was condemned to perpetual confinement at Bicêtre.

Let us compare this with a case seen recently on the psychiatric ward of one of our local general hospitals.

Marie, a 17-year-old girl, was admitted at three o'clock one morning following an overdose of 70 mgs. of Valium and other medicines. On admission she was drowsy but otherwise none the worse for her experience. Marie was the eldest of three children, a poor eater as an infant and rather lazy as a young child, but little else was reported of her early development that was unusual. In school she had trouble getting along with friends, tended to stare out the window, and there were

indications of some learning problems. In the sixth
grade she would not "settle down" and began to see the
guidance counselor because of her school problems.
School ended for her in the ninth grade at the age 15
when she ran off with her boyfriend who was sent to jail
where he later hung himself. Soon after this episode
she was admitted to a private mental hospital where she
went on a four-month rampage of stormy, violent behavior, wrist slashing, drug taking, alcohol abuse,
running away, defiance, and negativism. She was discharged as untreatable.

At age 16, about a year before her admission to the
general hospital unit, she became pregnant by a boy
whom she decided not to marry. In December, two months
prior to admission, she delivered a baby boy who was
born without a fibula and other more minor congenital
defects. Much of her anger and tension related to the
baby's care, which she neglected. Struggles with her
mother over who was to take care of the infant inten-
sified, and she was admitted to the hospital in the context of resolution of this conflict about the baby. She
had been in the hospital for several weeks when I was
asked to see her (she refused to come into the conference room), and was described by the staff as "murder."
On the ward she evinced an explosive temper, was verbally abusive, threatening to the staff, disruptive to
the patient community, and flaunted most of the rules.
The slightest thwarting of her wishes would lead to a
stream of insults and four-letter words, with an un-
failing instinct for finding a sore spot in another
person's style or personality. The staff described her
as like a wild animal, and she was running them ragged.
Efforts to have her take responsibility for the decisions about her baby, the meaning of its congenital
defects, or any reference to painful feelings or difficult aspects of her life would lead to avoidance and more
impulsive behavior. But when she was not riled up, the
ward staff said that Marie could be quite sweet and se-
ductive, even empathic with others and could talk en-
gagingly on a variety of subjects.

Although these two patients lived at different times and
consequently developed in environments of widely different
economic circumstances, social behaviors, and normative ex-

pectations, a number of important similarities are present.
Both individuals demonstrated marked emotional lability.
Each could easily change from a charming, competent, and
compassionate person to an enraged person. This rage was
not constrained by either social convention or regard for
other individuals. Although the fury seemed uncontrolled
and the individual appeared to be out of control, there was
no evidence of psychosis. Both were cases of "mania without
madness."

In the early nineteenth century, building on the work
of Pinel, James Cowles Prichard developed the concept of
"moral insanity" (1837). He held that this condition ranged
across a broad spectrum of disorders, including what we now
call the impulse or the character disorders--disorders in
which problems with the passions, the will, or the temperament are foremost and reason remains for the most part intact. Introduction of the concept of moral insanity into
the general field of insanity produced in this country a
well-documented controversy. The basic conflict was between
those who were willing to consider people with moral insanity
as sick and those who felt that they were simply bad. Isaac
Ray was a prominent exponent of the first position, while
John P. Gray, Superintendent of the Utica State Asylum, was
an effective spokesman for the second. This controversy
raged in the psychiatric literature of the mid-nineteenth
century in this country. In 1858 Gray wrote in an article
in the American Journal of Insanity (now the American Journal
of Psychiatry):

> The first recorded case of homicide, and it was a fra-
> tricide too, was committed by the first born of mankind
> against the second born. Were it not for the fact that
> God himself had judged the case, and imposed its penalty,
> thereby precluding all cavil and subtleties, the in-
> genious mind of a lawyer, physician, or psychologist of
> the present day, might make a more plausible argument
> from the face of the record, in favor of the moral in-
> sanity of Cain, than has lately been presented in favor
> of any man who has been accused of crime, and in whose
> defense the plea of moral insanity has been urged. . . .
> When the passions get the victory, as they are very apt
> to do, according to St. Paul, some modern judges and
> doctors are disposed to attribute it to moral insanity,
> while it is simply an ornate depravity. . . We cannot,

therefore, concur in recognizing as physical disease, without clear absolute proof of its being such, after a most thorough examination by the most thorough experts, any distinctive form of insanity that is so liable to disorganize and nullify the total criminal law as moral insanity is. It is elastic enough, if well stretched to cover every possible shade and degree of criminality, that has not a transparent guilty motive. It has already been made a cloak for homicide, arson, theft, lying, and drunkenness, under characteristic, though somewhat barbarous technical terms. It has almost protected the most conventional of all crimes, forgery; and probably would have done so if the dead languages could have supplied a proper sounding phrase to describe such a novel form of mania, and it would delude courts and juries into a belief that such a phrase implied scientific or psychological discovery to take the guilt out of sin, and convert crime into innocence; which, we conclude is the ultimate result of the doctrine of moral insanity.

We might breathe a sigh of relief and say that such mid-nineteenth century debates are at an end. Although we are now more enlightened about the need for collaborative work among the helping professions, law, religion, and other social institutions, I think we all recognize how much liveliness some of these issues still possess.

Darwin dealt another serious blow to the objective considerations of these disorders when he demonstrated that human beings were descended from the apes. In response to this insult to collective narcissism, a theory of mental illness called degeneration arose. This theory, as promulgated by Benedict Augustin Morel and those who followed him, declared that if indeed we are all descended from the apes, some of us, such as the insane and, above all, the deviants and delinquents, are more like the apes than others. An Italian criminologist, Cesare Lombroso (1911) attempted a thoroughgoing documentation setting out to prove that certain people, especially criminals, had atavistic characteristics (defined in terms of physical anomalies of their heads and bodies), demonstrating that of all mankind these individuals were closest to the lower animals and evinced "ferocious instincts." Against this background the concept of the psychopathic personality evolved. Individuals described as

psychopathic were considered physically and psychologically
less developed or more primitive--closer to lower phylogene-
tic forms--than other human beings.

This species of socioevolutionary theory was thought
to capture the spirit if not the laws of Darwin's revolu-
tion. The legacy it engendered continued to influence the
training in our institutions until the 1950s, and has perhaps still not been completely abandoned. Within this framework anyone who had an impulse disorder was simply labeled
a psychopath and was declared an inappropriate case for treatment, regardless of the particular mental institution in
which he or she happened to be. It was never quite clear
in fact which institution was appropriate for treating such
cases.

When psychoanalysis or dynamic psychiatry first brought
its insights and approaches to bear on the study and treatment of impulsive patients, these disturbances were considered among the psychopathic disorders. The concept of
character or personality only began to be of interest at
all to psychoanalysis in the first decade of this century
as a result of Freud's observations on the relationship
between certain instincts and particular personality traits.
In his paper "Character and Anal Erotism," Freud (1908)
demonstrated that particular traits, like parsimony or or-
derliness, are regularly associated with specific "anal
impulses." Freud also noted three possible fates that an
instinct may have: (1) it can be transformed into its opposite, which he called reaction formation; (2) it may be
sublimated; or (3) it can be given direct expression as a
force or drive. It is with this last manifestation of instincts in relation to impulses that we are most directly
concerned. During this period in the development of psychoanalytic theory and for many years afterward, the "character" of an individual was of concern only as it indicated
the form taken by "resistance" to treatment--an association
elaborated on extensively by Wilhelm Reich and later by
Anna Freud.

With the publication of Freud's The Ego and the Id
(1923), however, serious attention in psychoanalytic theory
began to focus on the structure of personality as such.
After the publication of this classical monograph, the history of our present thinking about impulse or character dis-

orders from the standpoint of dynamic psychiatry really
begins. Franz Alexander (1930), in his article "The Neurotic
Character," described people who externalize their conflicts
and draw society into their difficulties. He used Freud's
model of the neuroses and the familiar oedipal conflict,
but he saw in the society the representation of the internal
authority of the father. Alexander distinguished between
alloplastic individuals (those who act out their conflicts
toward the society) and autoplastic persons (those who retain
their conflicts within themselves as symptoms).

    Of still greater importance is the work of Wilhelm
Reich, which has not received nearly the attention it deserves
in this area. Reich wrote and published in 1925, shortly
after publication of The Ego and the Id, his classic work
Der Triebhafte Charakter--the impulsive character. This work
was not translated into English until 1970 (partly I think
because of Reich's fall into disrepute resulting from his
later odd theories), and then only in the Reichian Journal
of Orgonomy. It was 1974 before a translation of this work
was readily available. It is now recommended reading for
all students of the theory and treatment of impulsive behavior. Reich wrote that some individuals were uninhibited
in their impulses, both aggressive and sexual, and suffered
from a defect of repression. The problem, he said, lay in
the pathological development of the ego and superego, and
many of Reich's observations and questions anticipate issues
under consideration by contemporary theoreticians and clinicians. He postulated, for example, that

        an environment marked by scanty impulse control makes
        for poor ego ideal formation in the child, and, on the
        other hand, allows the impulse frustration to be more
        brutal than necessary. Hence the typically acute and
        outspoken ambivalence of the impulsive who can rightly
        say he was not taught any differently.

    Reich, as well as August Aichhorn, who worked with de-
linquent patients and was writing at about the same time
(1925), described the fatherless homes, the births out-of-
wedlock, the early orphanage, and inadequate mothering as
important elements leading to the development of impulsive
character problems. These factors, as well as the case
histories that give them substance, resemble those described
by contemporary investigators. Reich raised crucial issues
such as the "great value [in ascertaining] whether and to what

degree a constant change of nurturers weakens the defensive mechanisms. One might readily postulate that frequent changes in child-rearing practices produce a fragmentation and disorganization of ego ideals." Much subsequent work in this field and themes under current consideration concerning mother-infant relationships, problems in early identification, narcissistic injury, primitive defenses, conflicts over self-esteem, and impaired ego ideal formation are anticipated in Reich's work.

The importance of diagnosis in this area remains crucial. Impulsiveness, after all, is very common behavior. It occurs at one time or another in all of us and may even be adaptive. We have not talked about healthy impulsivity--spontaneity, for example, which is one form of it. What is the real differentiation between healthy, spontaneous, or adaptive impulsivity and the more troublesome kind that we focus on? Those investigating the social and environmental parameters of individual behavior pursue this question, but again I think it deserves more attention. One patient, with whom I am familiar, was helped very much with her impulsivity through psychotherapy. But she complained that the peaks and valleys of excitement and pleasure in life, those rhythms that she had previously experienced while she was "impulsive," were gone. In their place was a kind of monotony in her existence, even though she was "healthier," or at least less impulsive; though better adapted, she longed in some respects for her former life.

Jack Frosch in a recent paper (1977) attempted a diagnostic classification of the impulsive disorders, dividing them into two large categories. Disturbances in the first category are manifest by those individuals whose impulsivity takes the form of symptomatic acts. In these persons the impulse finds its expression in isolated acts which occur in response to a particular feeling or situation. The result is, for example, a sudden outburst of anger, or a particular sexual act expressing something specific in the background of the individual. Certain sexual deviations and kleptomania would be examples of what Frosch calls symptomatic impulsive expressions. The second major group comprises cases that, by and large, current investigation emphasizes--the character impulse disorders or impulse-ridden personalities for whom impulsivity permeates the whole character and for whom intolerance of anxiety or frustration is so prominent.

Differentiations such as Frosch's are important if advances are to be made in the understanding and treatment of impulse disorders. It is a mistake, for example, to assume that a particular act of violence reflects simply loss of control or poor ability to tolerate frustration (character impulse disorder). Some impulsive acts are quite focused in their motivation, or are the product of quite specific disturbances of ego development (symptomatic impulse disorders). It is essential for future progress in the understanding of impulsive acts that careful attention be given to all of the factors involved, including the developmental history, character structure, and personal psychodynamics of the individual "actor" and the social context or circumstances under which the so-called impulsive behavior occurred. Some murderous acts, for example, such as attempted assassination, may be carefully planned and deliberately carried out, and are impulsive only in the sense that sanction for a violent impulse was ultimately permitted by the superego. Other behavior, such as a tendency of a young man to get into frequent brawls, may reflect a more fundamental incapacity to plan, control, or delay impulsive expression.

Although work throughout the field of impulsive behavior and treatment has broadened considerably in recent years, several areas seem to warrant greater emphasis. We need to focus more on the relationship of impulsivity to biological differences in human beings that can begin to be observed in infancy as variations of temperament. The work of Margaret Fries, Berry Brazelton, and Chess and Thomas come to mind in this regard. Violent outbursts both in children and adults have been shown to occur following various forms of encephalitis, and EEG findings suggestive of thalamic and hypothalamic disturbances have been found to be associated with certain impulse disorders (Frosch, 1977). Such findings have important implications for the choice of drug treatment--such as the use of dilantin in impulse disorders where an associated EEG dysrhythmia has been discovered, or the selective use of tranquilizers and lithium in other types of impulse disturbances. We also need to pay greater attention to the relationship of adolescent and adult impulse disorders to childhood behavior patterns such as hyperactivity or learning difficulties such as dyslexia.

In addition, there is need for careful study of the developmental processes whereby the ability to delay grati-

fication is acquired. How do we learn the capacity for what
popular singer Carly Simon calls "Anticipation"? Do developmental functions, in addition to language development and the
maturation of cognitive structures, play major roles?

In the area of information-sharing, widespread need
exists for more intensive teaching and dissemination of knowledge among professionals throughout the entire field. However, I am particularly concerned about the need for more
specific and practical information for people whose daily
work is focused on the impulsive patient--for police, corrections officers, and paraprofessionals who carry much of the
burden that these patients place upon the society and its
institutions.

Other considerations exist which I do not know how to
categorize. Whereas symptom neuroses and to a large extent
psychoses are accepted by and large as the exclusive province
of mental health professionals, problems related to impulsivity bring us into territories which we share with others.
Most of the disorders under current scrutiny create significant social problems and we are not the only contributors
to their solution. We share this endeavor with the criminal
justice system, with educational systems, and with other
agencies and institutions of society. In some instances,
to be sure, the society is only too glad to have us take
over. Alcoholism, for example, has been declared a disease
and some have accepted this concept. But it remains a social
problem beyond the disease category. Drug addiction and
criminal violence are other areas that do not belong to the
mental health professions alone. Whatever our own views or
theories may be, we must work collaboratively with people
who have different assumptions and viewpoints, and perhaps
other priorities, than our own. New frontiers are beginning
to be approached through such collaborations in the fields
of child abuse or neglect, for example.

Another area calling for attention concerns the destructive expression of impulses in political life, terror imposed
upon societies from above by leaders, or expressions of the
impulsive side of man for particular purposes. Terrorism is
a special case in which hostile impulses are directed to the
redressing of vague or specific grievances. Psychiatrists
have been consulted with increasing frequency to provide
alternatives to impulsive retaliation in the handling of

terroristic incidents. Whether we are comfortable with this
role or not, psychiatrists will be called upon in the future
to bring their special skills and knowledge to areas where
they contribute with others in dealing with problems created
by man's impulsive nature.

Disturbing questions remain: Are there processes in contemporary life that encourage impulsivity in the society at
large—a general tendency toward immediacy of action for
prompt gratification? (Recent research suggests that for
those generations raised on TV, certain cognitive structures
in the brain have been shortcircuited—that, in fact, this medium may have had an actual effect on neurological development.) Are the predictions of Toffler and other futurists
valid in which they envision a society where delay will be
unnecessary and impulsivity more adaptive? (Will the impulsive personality inherit the earth?) And finally: What are
the roles and functions of the caring and allied professions
in dealing with these problems, as well as those encountered
through the continuing and often unplanned consequences of
social trends?

References

Alexander, F. 1930. The neurotic character. Int. J. of
    Psychoan., 11, 292-311.
Freud, S. 1908. Character and Anal Erotism. Standard Edi-
    tion of the Psychological Works of Sigmund Freud.
    Vol. IX, 167-175. London: Hogarth Press, 1959.
Freud, S. The Ego and the Id. 1923. Standard Edition of
    the Psychological Works of Sigmund Freud. Vol. XIX,
    3-66. London: Hogarth Press, 1961.
Frosch, J. 1977. The relation between acting out and dis-
    orders of impulse control. Psychiatry, 40, 295-314.
Gray, J. P. 1858. Moral insanity. Amer. J. of Insanity,
    14, 311-322.
Lombroso, Ferrero G. 1911. Criminal Man according to the
    Classification of Cesare Lombroso. New York: G.P.
    Putnam.
Pinel, Philippe. 1962. A Treatise on Insanity (transl. by
    D.D. Davis). New York: Hafner.

Prichard, J.C.   1837.   Treatise on Insanity and Other Dis-
    orders Affecting the Mind.   Philadelphia: E.L. Cary
    and A. Hart.
Reich, W.   1974.   The Impulsive Character and Other Writings.
    New York: New American Library.

INDEX